HOW TO BE
YOURSELF

Learn To Love Yourself, Build Meaningful Relationships, And Be The Best Person You Can Be

JOHN FERNANDO

TABLE OF CONTENTS

Introduction

I grew up as the only surviving child of two people with huge hearts. My dad was deaf and mute, so, it was assumed that he would never get married and have a family of his own. I found this out when we met one of my grandparents' friends. He was so surprised to be introduced to Raul's wife and son; they asked: "What, somebody actually married him?"

I was too young to feel insulted on behalf of my dad, but I guess I felt upset enough about it to remember it to this day. So yes, my dad overcame his limiting disabilities, exceeded expectations, got married, and had me. I am proud to be his son. He was also very proud of me. He would always point to me when he was with his friends, then point to himself with a smug look, clearly stating, "That kid over there is MY SON!"

My mom brought five children into this world, but only one survived - me. I don't know the details of how each of my siblings didn't make it. I was too small then to remember, but I remember a time when my mom had to be away for a few weeks, and I had to stay with my aunt after she gave birth to one of my siblings. I was also sent away to my grandma's in another province because of superstition. I was apparently the reason that my siblings didn't survive, and in order for them to successfully have another child, I had to be away during the process.

I was very much loved and treasured because I was the only child of two people who couldn't have any other children. My mom gave me all her attention and gave in to most of my demands at home. My dad, after making his "statement," would call me over to hand me some money for all to see, including all the other kids in the neighborhood.

My dad handed me ten or even sometimes twenty-peso paper bills when all the other kids would feel very lucky if they were given a single peso coin. My life as a kid was relatively effortless compared to most kids who grew up in my old neighborhood. I had almost everything I needed handed to me by my parents, and I never had to work hard for anything that I wanted. Most kids in my neighborhood had to help with household chores like cooking or getting water from the nearby water pump to earn their keep. Me? – The most work I had to do was the occasional tantrum I had to pull for my mom to get me some toy I wanted. I know, I was a spoiled brat. Go ahead and hate me.

In our neighborhood, I was the kid with the nicest toys. I had robots and legos while all the other kids could only build toys out of discarded milk cans and bamboo.

I was that annoying rich kid to my childhood friends. Just to make it very clear, we aren't rich. In fact, my dad's income was from the few hundred dollars each month that he got from social security. It would easily put us in the low poverty line here in the US, but from where I came from, those same few hundred dollars were enough to give us a more comfortable life than most of our neighbors.

Aside from being the annoying rich kid, I also was the naïve kid. Because the other kids knew I had a lot of money and how naïve I was, some kids frequently talked me into buying them snacks and other stuff.

I'm not saying it was all of them, but certain kids took advantage of the situation. There was this older kid who would even ask for all my money and used it all to buy ramen. Then, he'd have us hide in the middle of the sugarcane fields while we cook then eat the ramen. When I asked him why we had to hide, he told me it was because he didn't want the other kids to take advantage of me. I believed him of course. What I didn't realize was that he was the one who was taking the most advantage of me. Essentially, my childhood became all about my "friends" asking me to buy them stuff. They were paying attention to me only to borrow my stuff or get me to buy them snacks. If I didn't have the goods, I was nobody to them.

I'm not saying everyone took advantage of me. I'm saying this now because I don't want to go back home to my old neighborhood and have my house surrounded by people with torches and pitchforks when word reaches them about what I wrote here. All I'm saying is that some kids did, and I was blind to all of it.

I spent a great deal of time believing that it was simply how things worked, that people only liked people who gave them what they wanted.

Because my childhood friends seemed only to like me when I was useful to them, I grew up believing that people only liked me when I gave them something they wanted.

Who doesn't want to be liked? I wanted people to like me. I was used to having a lot of attention at home from my parents, so I wanted a lot of attention outside my home as well. I gave what my friends wanted because I wanted them to like me and to pay attention to me.

Fast forward to my first year in college. Sitting alone in the middle of an empty classroom with nobody to hang out with, I asked myself, where did I go wrong?

I tried to act cool and tried to give people what I thought they wanted, so why was I all alone?

Why didn't I feel like I belonged anywhere when I tried my very best to please everyone?

It was around that time that I decided to start a journal. I thought that I should start documenting my thoughts and feelings during those times of loneliness, hoping that it would help me to have a better understanding of myself and what I was feeling.

I eventually learned to stop caring about what other people thought about me. I figured out that it didn't matter how I looked or how I acted; there's just no point in trying too hard to please everyone. More importantly, I figured out that I didn't have to make people like me. - That I could be happy even if nobody else liked me. If nobody wanted to be my friend, I could be my own friend. If nobody liked me, I could like myself. I don't need anyone else to love me, because I can love myself.

After some time, the funniest thing happened: I started getting real friends who liked me for who I was, who didn't need me to give them anything or do anything for them.

This is my story of learning the hard way how to be myself and how being myself brought me the happiness and company that I've always wanted. Fortunately, if you have this book, you can learn to be yourself and be happy too, minus the hard way. I am putting myself out there and at some points, embarrassing myself by telling you about some of my biggest mistakes, so that you can see that you're not the only one going through some real shit and that there's always hope no matter how bad it gets. It's not easy to learn to be yourself when you've been so used to pretending to be something else, but it's certainly worth the effort.

I went through a lot of experiences in life that taught me lesson after lesson until I realized how important it is to truly be myself. I will try my best to be as entertaining and informative as I can in order to teach you about all the lessons I have learned. My hope is that through this book, you will learn why you need to learn to be yourself, how you can find and express yourself, and how being yourself impacts your life and your relationships.

I've also made a quick instructional guide to help you make a great first impression and start meaningful conversations. You can get it at no extra cost at https://johnfernando.com.

So, are you ready to change your life in amazing ways? Let us dive in.

CHAPTER 1

Learn To Love Yourself

I grew up in the Philippines and over at my old neighborhood, people always assumed that my family had a lot of money. Technically, they were right because my dad was an American immigrant and got a regular monthly stipend of a few hundred dollars from Social Security. I don't know exactly what the details are, but I know that he worked in the fields of Salinas, California for a while. This allowed him to collect a monthly amount worth just a few hundred dollars. Nothing impressive, especially here in the US but in the Philippines, those few hundred dollars went a really long way, and we lived a comfortable life compared to most of our neighbors.

My dad was generous with everyone, and he always made a show of giving me a lot of money in public. He would call me over while I was playing with the other kids and hand me ten or even twenty-peso bills for everyone to see. Back then, the other kids would consider themselves lucky if their parents even gave them a single peso. This very public show did a few things to me as a kid that I realize now:

First, it made me believe that money was easy.

Second, every kid in our neighborhood knew I had a lot of money.

Third, because I had a lot of money, some kids decided to take advantage of me.

Essentially, some of the friends I thought I had as a kid only wanted me for the free snacks. When I couldn't get them anything, they didn't pay attention to me. So, I developed this mentality that I needed to give my "friends" what they wanted so they'd keep liking me and would stay friends with me. This was, of course, not a good thing for a kid or for any person to think. I didn't know any better, and I allowed this to continue for many years because I really thought this was the way the world worked.

I also grew up being given too much love by my parents. I have never seen my parents work for our money, and they also gave me almost everything I wanted, so I didn't understand the real value of money. I was given all the attention I ever wanted. I was always the best because well, there was nobody else to compare me to because I'm the only child they got. This gave me an abnormally high opinion of myself.

Having a high opinion of myself made me expect certain things from everyone else. I expected everyone to pay attention to me all the time and not to give me a hard time when there was something I wanted. I, therefore, expected my friends to pay attention to me all the time, and I wanted them to think that I'm the best. When some of them turned out to just want things from me, I decided that giving them what they wanted from me was the path of least resistance to getting the attention and admiration I wanted.

Just to be clear, I'm not blaming my parents. They did what they thought was best. And, if I tried to have kids five times and all but one survived, I would really give my all to the one that survived. Heck, as I'm writing this now, I have one child, and I'm already spoiling her enough.

Also, I'm not blaming my childhood friends. We were kids. I was selfish for wanting a lot of attention, and I was too naïve to say no. I wanted friends, and they wanted snacks and toys. In a way, we got what we wanted from each other.

As I grew up a little more, I was sent to the best school in the province where the other kids had parents who were also well off financially and so the other kids there also had the same things I had if not better. I quickly discovered that there was little that I could offer the other kids in terms of snacks because they had their own snacks too, and most of them even had better snacks than I did.

I quickly discovered that the game was played a little different in this field. Back in my neighborhood, I had the advantage of simply having more resources than everyone else. In this school, I couldn't use my resources as an advantage because there were a lot of kids who had more than I did. So, the game became about who looked cool or who did the things that everyone else thought was cool. Basically, it became a game of politics – swaying public opinion.

If you knew me when I was in elementary and high school, you probably would find me as one of the most annoying people you could ever know. I tried a lot of stunts that I thought would make my peers think that I was a cool guy. If I saw someone who was more awesome than I was, I would do my best to copy them because I wanted everyone to see how awesome I was too.

The problem then, was that I was playing the game wrong because I had a false understanding of the rules. I thought that being cool was all about acting self-assured like you didn't have a care in the world – essentially, projecting self-confidence. What I didn't realize, was that acting like you were cool wasn't what made you self-confident. Instead, being confident was what made you naturally cool. Basically, the real cool guys had self-confidence and weren't desperate for attention like I was. They were sure about themselves, so they just did whatever they wanted, and that made them cool. They didn't worry about what other people thought of them as I did.

The funny thing was that on the outside, I did my best to appear cool and confident, but on the inside, I kept doubting myself and questioned if what I was doing was cool enough. I always worried about what my image was and whether people were paying attention to the cool things I was doing. I had high expectations of myself, and of course, I always ended up being disappointed. Because of my consistent failure to meet the expectations I set for myself, I eventually developed a negative inner voice.

Your Inner Voice

It's natural for people to criticize themselves. We are our own worst critic as we know ourselves better than anyone else. The imperfections or the mistakes that we let our inner critic beat us up over are often not even noticed by the people around us. The funny thing is that we do this mostly because we hold ourselves to a higher standard than other people.

When you let yourself feel that you are not good enough, you could get stuck in a cycle of negative thinking and self-hatred. This could eventually lead to you developing what we would refer to as your negative inner voice. This that voice inside your head that keeps putting you down and reminding you of all your mistakes and all the things that are ugly about you.

If you continue to listen to your negative inner voice, you might start to believe it when it tells you that you are stupid or embarrassing. It will continue to go unchecked as you will stop challenging these dangerous ideas that come across your head. You could start to feel helpless and start to believe that this is the way that life is or the way things are and that there is no way to change these "truths" about yourself. Your self-esteem and confidence then take a blow, and you may begin to withdraw yourself from people.

In some cases, instead of withdrawing, you might instead take the opposite approach and start to present your outer self as superior to other people. You are doing this for the simple fact that you want to be accepted, but most of the time, it may just cause people to dislike or resent you. This is a defense mechanism that is used to avoid the internal voice speaking negatively, as it usually starts when there is any sign of failure. This was what happened to me. I started to project an image that I was cool and ended up alienating people.

It is almost second nature for people to present themselves in the best light possible, even as children. We learn from an early age that people-pleasing gets us special attention, gifts, and unique privileges. As a result, we learn that this is what relationships with other people are built on, when in fact, it is just an interaction. If we continue to be people-pleasers because of a desire to be liked and to avoid criticism, we carry these same patterns into adulthood, and we continue to listen to the negative inner voice leading us along the way.

As an example, when you are performing actions that may not be in your best interest, such as having another drink when you're already drunk, your conscience will tell you that you should consider not having another. However, your negative inner voice could trick you into making the decision to have another drink because not having that next drink could make you look weak, only for it to berate you later for making that decision when you wake up the next day hungover.

As another example, you may have had an argument with a loved one that did not end very well. Your conscience will tell you that you need to resolve the matter with them in a civil manner, whereas your negative inner voice will convince you that you were justified in your actions, or alternatively, it may nag you about how you screwed up the entire relationship because of this one fight.

What Causes You to Hate Yourself?

Sometimes, it is difficult to pinpoint the exact root cause of negative thought processes without digging deep. The causes are going to be different for each person and experienced at differing levels. However, there are some common causes which result in hating oneself.

Environment and Upbringing during Childhood

When a person in a state of self-hatred, it sometimes stems from feelings of inadequacy during childhood when they were trying to cope with the environment in which they were brought up and with their parent's style of acceptance, love, and discipline which all play a role in how they are able to accept themselves as well as how they present themselves to the world.

As children are more sensitive to different emotions and circumstances, they tend to feel the emotions of their caregivers on a stronger level. If those feelings are of a negative nature, a child may feel threatened when their parents are angry, even if it is not directed solely at them. These negative instances impact their memories even more than the times their parents were loving towards them.

If this has occurred over a long period of time, this could lead them to feel neglected. The way that their parents or caregivers have subconsciously taught them to act will also likely lead them having a low opinion of themselves. If they were made to feel undeserving of love, useless, or worthless as a child, these beliefs could stay with them as they continue to grow into adulthood unless measures are taken to dismantle these false beliefs and thoughts.

Emotionally-Traumatic Experiences

These instances can occur during any part of a person's life and result in impactful shifts in the way that they view themselves in general. When a person experiences emotional trauma, it can cause a ripple effect that not only affects their mental or emotional health at the time of the trauma, but it can also reach into years or even decades afterward.

These events could lead a person to question who they are, or even who they might be in the future. Traumatic events come in many forms such as sudden bereavement, violent or sexual attacks, acts of terrorism, natural disasters, or an accident. What makes it worse is that these memories and experiences are swept under the rug, never to be talked about or dealt with.

This is why it is sometimes difficult to pinpoint these impactful experiences when they happen during early childhood as they can be buried within the psyche. When you are digging deeper into the root cause of your issues, it may be wise to talk to family members about these matters. Even though it may be delicate and very painful for them to bring up, you must urge them that talking about these instances openly without judgment will help bring closure for you to move past these experiences so that you can live your life in a healthier way.

Chemical Imbalances

If a person suffers from general depression or any other psychological conditions, their self-hate may be linked to a chemical imbalance. This can be due to a genetic factor or something induced by physical trauma or substances such as medications or illicit drugs.

The best way to know if you are experiencing this type of problem is to visit your doctor to get medically tested. It can be a hard step to acknowledge that mental illness may be the root of your negative inner voice, but it is best to have all of the information so that you can make educated decisions on how to proceed. Being born with this imbalance does not automatically mean that you have to let it continue to be an obstacle for you to change your mindset.

Being Bullied

When a person is constantly attacked by a bully, this could have a direct impact on one's self-concept. Usually, being bullied chips away at any self-worth that a person may have. No matter if their abuse is physical or in the form of harsh words, they often will scar a person for many years. The experience of being bullied could have a huge impact on the mental and physical well-being of the victim.

When the bully is able to continue with their attack and succeed in breaking down their victim's self-worth, oftentimes, the victim will start to believe everything the bully is saying because they do not hear anything different to refute the bully's claims. The sad part is that the abuse could remain with a person for a long time and undermine their sense of self-worth.

It's easy to think of bullies as people you find during school or on the playground, but this is not necessarily the case. They can be found in family members, romantic relationships, so-called friends, or even in the workplace. A bully can be of any age, and they are extremely toxic people to be around. If you think this may be the cause of your self-hatred, break ties, or at least minimize contact with this person while you are in the healing stage.

Regrets

I had a lot of regrets, and I made sure to spend most of my time thinking about all the things I regretted. It made me feel miserable, and I would struggle to hold back my tears. Sometimes it would get so bad that I would have trouble sleeping, have difficulty breathing, or get headaches.

One day, it just hit me. Why was I tormenting myself over things that I couldn't change?

It's not like I have a time machine. I don't know anyone else who has one either. No matter how miserable I make myself feel, there is nothing I can do to change anything that has happened in the past.

All I was doing was torturing myself for nothing. I was using up my precious time and energy, thinking about things that won't improve my life or my situation. Instead of using my time and energy on things that could get me moving forward, I had been holding myself back and dragging myself down with my past.

Has anything like my experience ever happened to you? Have you been dwelling on your past mistakes and torturing yourself with your regrets? Has any of it ever helped you improve things?

Some life experiences can bring about regret, especially when a person has been treated by another person in an unfair way or when a person commits a serious mistake with big, adverse consequences.

Other instances could include opportunities that you wish you had taken as you may feel you would be in a much better place right now if only you had done this or that.

Of course, it is only natural to feel remorse when you were in the wrong. However, the healthier way to go about "fixing" regrets is to come to a resolution with the people who you may have wronged in the past. If it was a lost opportunity, look for other ways to better your life through new experiences. Sometimes, all you need to do is get to the point where you can forgive and forget about these regrets. What is done is done. You need to let these thoughts go as the path of negative thinking will only sink you further into your self-loathing state.

Signs of Self-Loathing

When you find yourself being berated by your negative inner voice, it is never in your best interest to keep this dialogue rolling in your mind. After some time, it starts to affect the way that you behave and think, which is detrimental to your mental health.

Below are several signs of self-loathing that you have to watch out for:

- Comparing yourself to other people

- Strongly agreeing with criticism and ignoring any praise

- Over- or under-eating

- Careless about personal hygiene

- Defeatist attitude

- Being a martyr for attention

- Unnecessary spending

- Isolation

- Drug or alcohol abuse

- Deliberate relationship sabotage

- Refuse to acknowledge there is a problem or get help

Comparing Yourself to Other People

It is natural to compare yourself to other people. It helps you to learn how to act in social situations and makes you feel a little more sure about your place. However, when you focus solely on what other people are doing with their lives, you lose out on the opportunity to live your own life.

This is a dangerous cycle as you become anxious or even frightened about going outside of the invisible lines of what is acceptable in society. It makes you scared of taking risks, and you start to become obsessed about what other people will think of you if you step out of the defined norm.

If you are not able to be comfortable with staying within these accepted ideas of society, you could start to hate yourself. This is the result of the presumption that because you are seeing other people who you presume to be on the same level as you perform well and succeed, you should be able to achieve the same level of success. If you don't, then you might start to think that something is inherently wrong with you for not being able to do the same. This is the ugly result of comparing yourself to other people.

Strongly Agreeing with Criticism and Ignoring any Praise

When you do not have a high view of yourself, you are likely not able to take in moments where people are praising you. It feels uncomfortable because you do not feel like you deserve these compliments, even when you know deep down that you did something worthy of the praise you are receiving. You might not know how to handle these compliments because they cause friction with how you feel about yourself on the inside.

On the other hand, when someone criticizes you, this feels more comfortable as it is how you feel inwardly towards yourself. This is easier to comprehend as it feels more natural because the negativity may have become ingrained in you. You are likely used to having negative dialogue run through your mind more often than not. It is certainly a red flag if you are able to accept criticism better than you do a compliment.

Over or Under-Eating

It is a common occurrence for you to have a love/hate relationship with food when you are in a state of self-hatred. This can manifest in many ways to include not eating enough, perhaps because you have a self-image issue or maybe you feel like you do not deserve to be nourished correctly. On the other hand, you may indulge too much in food to try to smother the negative thoughts you have about yourself through the pleasure that food brings. Either behavior can lead to serious eating disorders, which could, in turn, lead to physical illness.

Care Less About Personal Hygiene

This symptom can take on several forms. When someone decides not to keep up their outer appearance or their personal hygiene, they often feel like they do not deserve to feel or look good.

This cycle can lead to more carelessness about personal appearance. Like many of the signs of self-hatred, they all continue to fuel the cycle. Because you do not look "good," it gives your inner voice an excuse to continue to put yourself down because you may believe that it's pointless even to try to look good.

Defeatist Attitude

This is a type of negative self-talk where you may be very capable of accomplishing a task, but your inner voice talks you out of it. Your inner self makes you believe that you are going to fail before you have even tried or that things will not work out because your skills are less than perfect.

Because this type of self-talk is giving the expectation of your failure, it reinforces your negative inner voice, driving you deeper into self-loathing. It is also a type of punishment for those who are not allowing themselves to experience any joy. Not only are you stripping yourself of good opportunities, but you are also missing out on opportunities to grow as an individual as you will never know if you are good at something until you try.

Being a Martyr for Attention

You may put yourself in the position of acting like a martyr or perform a noble act so that you can gain positive feedback and attention. This is usually a temporary way in which you can gain a sense of worth from other people. It can also act as a punishment to yourself as it is an act of sacrifice of your time and resources. Even if you receive the amount of praise and attention that you were seeking, you are likely to harm yourself in the process mentally or physically by pushing yourself further than necessary to receive the approval of other people.

Unnecessary Spending

Sometimes, when you feel unhappy on the inside, you may try to fill the void with material possessions. You may spend a lot of money or even get into debt for a collection or the latest gadgets so that you have something to feel good about, hoping that these material things will replace the self-hatred and shame that you may be feeling inside.

Sometimes, these items are not purchased for yourself but for others in an attempt to buy other people's appreciation and company. These types of gifts can range from cheap to expensive and are usually based on the amount of attention that you might want from the other person.

This plan sometimes backfires as it usually puts people off as they do not feel comfortable about the situation. However, it can work on those people who are taking advantage of your kindness as they will continue to receive these gifts while likely not giving much in return. In turn, this can lead you to feel worthless if the other party doesn't react the way you were expecting.

Isolation

When you are in a state of mind where you are feeling depressed or engaged in negative self-talk, you might try to isolate yourself. This can be because you do not feel like you belong within any social group or you have convinced yourself that everyone does not like you. The result of your isolation supports your inner voice by making you feel more alone and alienated from the world.

If there is an invite that you receive to go out, you are likely to consider this to be a pity invitation as your inner voice has convinced you they do not like or understand you. Many times you may complain about the state of your social life or wish things were different, but you are likely to not take any stand in making any changes about the situation. When you put yourself into isolation, you are going to continue to slide down into deeper negative self-talk, feeling sorry for yourself as you will have no one else's input to tell you anything positive.

Drug or Alcohol Abuse

When you are in a negative state of mind, it is common for you to want to numb, ignore, or even forget about the current state of affairs in your life. When you have emotions that are unwanted or uncomfortable to you, it is easy to use drugs or alcohol to temporarily disengage so that you do not have to deal with how you feel. Because of the common side effects of using these intoxicants, you are likely to feel the after-effects which also build upon strengthening your self-loathing feelings.

Because you may feed off of the shame, guilt, and overall negative physical feelings, you are likely to continue abusing these substances to continue to feel these effects. As you can imagine, this could be another dark cycle that can continue to spiral out of control.

Deliberate Relationship Sabotage

Many times you may feel like you are undeserving of feeling or receiving the good aspects of life such as kindness, beauty, or love, which are typically part of any good relationship. Because of this feeling of unworthiness, you might try to sabotage your own relationships when they are starting to go well or when the other person is getting too close for comfort.

This sabotage can take on many forms such as cheating on them, being verbally or physically abusive towards them, or generally mistreating them until they finally decide that they have had enough and leave you. Your negative inner voice could then convince you that you were justified in how you treated them because it makes you feel in control and that you won't let anyone have the power to hurt you.

You may also feel like you have more control over the situation when you are the one to abandon your partner so that you will not be unexpectedly hurt by them. Sometimes, you may even make yourself believe that you are setting your partner free of the inevitable pain, which is sure to occur by staying with you.

Refusing to Acknowledge There is a Problem or Get Help

It is difficult for some people to realize and accept that they are in need of help or that they have a problem. Admitting that you have issues sometimes feels very difficult because you're scared of being vulnerable, and even if you get to the point of realizing that you are in need of help, you might try to convince yourself that it is useless as nothing can help you.

For example, you may think about how a therapy session might help, but you predict the most negative outcome and do not entertain the possibility of any positive outcome. You're afraid to give anything a chance because you believe that it is likely to fail anyway because it's what your negative inner voice has told you.

How to Stop the Cycle of Self-Hatred

Just as you have a negative inner voice, you can start to develop a positive inner voice. Have you heard of the idea of becoming your own best friend? If you haven't heard of it before, then let me be the first to tell you that this is a real possibility as you can change your mindset to reflect this new relationship with yourself. It's of course not easy, and it could take some effort and time as you may have already been used to having your negative inner voice for a while. However, it is still doable and better than letting your negative inner voice constantly bring you down. The negative inner voice is something you learned, so it's also something you can unlearn. At the same time, you can learn to grow and develop your positive inner voice.

You can start by not listening too much to that negative inner voice that keeps bringing you down. Instead of paying attention to the negative thoughts in your head reminding you of all the painful mistakes that you might have done in the past, you could start thinking of all the good things that you've experienced. Instead of listening to the negative inner voice telling you how ugly or inadequate you are, you can instead try to find the good things about you because there are many, you just have to let yourself find them and recognize them.

When you find the determination to change your life for the better, little will stand in your way of realizing your goals. This is not to say that there will not be unforeseen challenges along the way, but with your new mindset, you will see these as opportunities to grow as a person.

You must accept that each person is uniquely different, and this is something that must be embraced. Even if it does not seem like it, everyone has imperfections they would rather keep to themselves. However, the most authentic people lay it out on the table for everyone who is worthy to see. There is no reason to hide behind the flaws that you possess. This is a fact of life that everyone has to come to terms with.

Yes, nobody is perfect. Some people are just better at hiding their imperfections than others. But, instead of just hiding your imperfections, I want you to try to embrace your imperfections. They are a part of you. Here, let me go first:

I have crooked teeth. I have a very poor fashion sense. I'm fat. I was a jerk who didn't have a sense of self-identity as a young man. I'm not attractive enough to be a model. I snore. I have done incredibly dumb things like jump off an antenna tower and caused embarrassment to my family. There. Some of my mistakes and flaws open to you, and it's all true. You'll see when you meet me or ask people from my hometown.

I used to do a half-smile where I cover my upper teeth just to hide my crooked teeth. But eventually, I realized that if a person doesn't like me just because of my ugly teeth then they're not worth my time anyway, so I started to accept it as a part of me. I know I said that we were relatively well-off compared to our neighbors from my hometown, but that didn't mean we were rich and could afford to get me braces. I used to get teased because of my teeth. Back when I worked at a clinic, I remember a kid loudly telling his mom to check out my teeth. It was funny because the mom was so much more embarrassed about the whole thing than I was.

The secret to me not being bothered about my teeth or about any of the things I just mentioned above? – Simple. I accept them as part of me. I am where I am because of all my flaws. Anyone who lets my flaws get in the way of them liking me isn't worth my time. I'm a good guy, and though I no longer think as highly of myself as I once did, I still know that I'm awesome in my own way and I can add value to the lives of people who can look past my imperfections.

My life is not perfect, but I'm working on it. I'm not attractive enough to be a model, but my girlfriend thinks I'm sexy and those who think I'm not worth their time aren't worth my time either. I was a jerk when I was younger, but I try my best to stay humble and write about my experiences to help people. I did try to kill myself before, but now I try to make my life benefit the people I love, as well as the people like you who I have touched in some way. I embrace all the ugly things about me because it's what gives contrast to the beautiful things that I try to be.

When you have this perspective on yourself, it puts you in a position to be able to love yourself fully and without regret. No matter what faults you feel like you have, you are still a human being who is worthy and deserving of love. There is nothing that should block you from embracing the authentic person that you are, as this is half the battle of living your life to the fullest.

Learning how to love yourself for who you really are may be a difficult task at first. No one wants to necessarily look in the mirror to see all of their flaws. If you have a negative perspective of yourself, don't give up. You have a whole life ahead of you to work on that. One way to make it easier is to have an accepting attitude with yourself.

No matter what your inner voice may be saying, ignore it unless you can substantiate its claims with actual evidence and even if there was evidence, it's not all that defines you as a person. Whatever mistakes you may have done in the past, you can atone and start making a positive impact on others by striving to do good and to be the best person you can be. Whoever you are and whatever you are, you deserve to be loved. If you think that nobody else could love you, then start by loving yourself. Show other people that you deserve to be loved by loving yourself, and the right ones will learn to love you as well.

CHAPTER 2

Overcome Social Anxiety and Shyness

I remember back in college, there was this shy girl whose name I've forgotten, primarily because she just stayed in a spot near the back corner of the classroom and never spoke to anyone.

One day, we were placed in random groups and asked to do a role-playing activity.

This girl simply refused to go in front of the class, no matter how much everyone tried to encourage her.

She was so afraid to be in front of the class that she eventually cried. This earned her no mercy from the professor, who told her that she would fail the activity if she didn't participate. Still, it wasn't enough to make her go to the front to play her part.

While I felt bad that she cried, back then, I didn't understand how she could be so afraid to go in front of the class that it would make her cry. I do understand the fear of embarrassing yourself in front of other people, but to feel such an intense fear that you'd rather get a failing mark and cry in public is something I couldn't understand.

In today's society, it is all too easy to get wrapped up in what other people think about us. We often mistakenly feel that how others perceive us is how we are defined as a person. This is of course not true, our exposure to the media where the standards of beauty are set at a very high bar and all the different things we see on TV and on the internet like the latest fashion trends, the latest tech, the glamorous lifestyles of celebrities – all these can sometimes make a person feel inadequate. It's been ingrained in many of us because society in general somehow teaches us to seek the approval of other people in order to fit in.

I know very much how that feels. I believe I mentioned it earlier in the book when I tried to imitate people who I thought were cool and popular because I also wanted to appear cool and become popular. I have always had a poor fashion sense. I always tend to mismatch things, and I just don't get what looks good and what doesn't most of the time. These days I just wear plain black or grey shirts, but back then I attempted to copy how actors on TV dressed up and how they styled their hair. Sometimes it worked, but most of the time it just doesn't seem to work for me. I wanted to look nice and fashionable, and while there's nothing wrong with wanting to look nice, my intentions were purely because I wanted to be praised for looking good and have people's attention.

Eventually, instead of caring too much about what other people think, I realized that what I really need to focus on is my individual needs, desires, cares, and goals. What other people think of me is really none of my business, and it's really something I can't control. What I can control, however, is what I think of myself, and that's what eventually gave me enough self-confidence to just express myself as I wanted.

I have to warn you that your social life will change too once you make the decision to just be yourself without caring about what other people think. Naturally, the people who relate to you and understand you will continue to be part of your life, while the ones that do not approve of the real you will fall out of your life. This can bring about stressful situations if you hold deep attachments and have long histories with these people. When the scenario comes about where someone who used to be close to you simply falls away because you "changed," you need to keep in mind that what you want is to express your real self and you want people who will accept you for who you really are. You need to keep your mind focused on your personal goals.

What Causes Extreme Shyness?

A lot of people may have a difficult time making friends due to shyness and find it hard to maintain a social life because of anxiety. According to Dr. Brian Cox, up to sixty percent of the adult population suffers from anxiety or shyness. Of course, there are people who are born being naturally shy, but this only applies to approximately fifteen percent (Bressert 2018).

While it is hard to pinpoint exactly what causes extreme shyness, there are certain known factors like genetics, a person's upbringing, and certain stressful situations that may contribute to the development of social anxiety and shyness.

Recent studies into specific genetic markers for social anxiety have narrowed it down to changes in a gene called SLCGA4. This specific gene is known to be primarily involved in the transport of a neurotransmitter called serotonin, which helps stabilize a person's mood, and people with social anxiety disorder seem to struggle to produce serotonin consistently.

In neurological studies, brain scans have revealed an association between the hyperactivity of the part of the brain called the amygdala and feelings of social anxiety. The amygdala is known for being the part of the brain controlling the fight-or-flight response which includes an elevated heart rate and excitability to name a few, which also happens to be similar to how a person with social anxiety feels when in a social setting.

Children whose parents are overcontrolling, quick to criticize, or are overly concerned with the opinions of others may develop fearfulness and mistrust of other people, and their self-esteem may also become negatively impacted. This, of course, may be carried by the child into adulthood.

Also, highly stressful or traumatic experiences such as being bullied or abused verbally, physically, or sexually also plays a big factor in damaging a person's self-esteem.

Tips On Overcoming Social Anxiety and Shyness

If you're suffering from social anxiety, one helpful exercise may be to look deep into your past to determine the cause of your beliefs about yourself. When you understand how you got to be shy and lacking the self-confidence you require, you may have a better understanding on how to best approach your issues. Try to pinpoint the reason why you want to avoid interacting with people or why you're scared to get into meaningful relationships with other people, and then you can start to figure out a way to properly address these issues. Depending on how serious your issues are, you may need to get help from a professional such as a therapist or a psychiatrist.

What I can tell you, however, is that sometimes your issues may all be in your head. I know it sounds like I'm downplaying it but based on the people I know who have suffered from social anxiety, their fears are usually unfounded like that girl in college who refused to go in front of the class. There wasn't anyone there who disliked her and nobody was out to get her. In fact, a lot of us discovered that day that we couldn't become actors because we sucked! There wasn't anything wrong with her physically, and she was wearing her uniform the same as us. There was nothing on the outside for her to be worried about. But of course, this is from someone on the outside. Inside her head, she must have been so afraid of something that we couldn't see. If you're suffering from social anxiety, if you can, try to gain control of your thoughts and try to see if your fears are real or if they're simply in your head.

It may also help to gradually expose yourself to the things that trigger your social anxiety. The keyword here is gradual. Don't try to do open mic nights on day one if you feel like it's too much. Just try crossing your comfort zone little-by-little each day and hope to accomplish more today than you did yesterday. That's advice that works for most things that you want to improve in your life and not only with social anxiety.

Even just a trickle of improvement as long as it's done in a regular and consistent manner really ads up and eventually you'll notice how far you've come.

Start out simple and light in your conversations with other people. There is no need to dive straight in because you will likely get overwhelmed and give up. You want to start with baby steps to build your confidence in speaking with other people. Also, remember that you can politely excuse yourself from the conversation if it is getting too much for you. Just keep engaging people and talk to them for as much as you can. Eventually, you'll develop the confidence to maintain and even enjoy conversing with other people.

Remember to be kind and understanding to yourself. Do not beat yourself up if you end up saying something embarrassing or something that people find upsetting.

Learning to love yourself with your strengths and weaknesses will help you appreciate the individual that you are, and that's why I placed it at the beginning of this book. Working on a list of attributes and strengths you possess will give you the insight that you require to help you overcome your shy feelings. When you focus on your strengths, you will feel more confident within yourself, and it will also help you deal with your weaknesses in a more constructive way.

Try to challenge and overcome your self-limiting thoughts. These are the thoughts you have that tell you that you can't do something or that you'll just end up failing. When you learn to challenge your self-limiting thoughts, you will find that your self-esteem will gradually build up as you start overcoming each challenge.

Make it an active choice every morning to wake up and become better today than yesterday. Of course, there are going to be setbacks but if you look at these obstacles as opportunities to learn rather than automatically classifying them as unsolvable mysteries, you will advance much more quickly, feeling better and more confident with yourself.

You will also find that many of the negative thoughts and beliefs that you have about yourself that make you self-conscious about how you look or act are usually not real. The things that you think are undesirable about you are often not even noticed or thought about by the people around you. Remember, your flaws are not written on your forehead. Normal people don't go around looking for ugly things about the people they're talking to.

It is also helpful to fully engage with other people in an authentic way. When you connect with someone on a deeper level, they are not going to care so much about how every hair on your head is not perfect or that you may be a little overweight. Genuine people will not care about these attributes and want to connect with the real person you are inside. Show people your value by valuing yourself. You're good, and you're gonna be fine. Go show the world how awesome you can be!

CHAPTER 3

Keep Moving Forward

I used to think a lot about when I was here in the US as a high school kid. My aunt gave me the choice to stay with them or to go back home to the Philippines with my dad. I believe that it's the single most important decision I have ever consciously made in my life.

I'm not sure about how things might have turned out if I'd chosen to stay with my aunt, but I know that things would have been very different for me if I had.

I probably wouldn't have met the mother of my daughter, which means I wouldn't have my daughter either. I probably would be doing something else, too, rather than writing my books.

At times, I would think about the dumb mistakes I made that I could have easily avoided if I only knew some minor thing.

Sometimes I would think about the night before my dad passed away. He was scheduled to have knee surgery the following morning. His arthritis got so bad on one knee that he was having a hard time putting weight on it and needed a walker. He was very anxious about the surgery, and over and over, he indicated that he didn't want to go through with it, that he just wanted to go back home to the Philippines.

I was trying to get him to eat dinner, but he refused to take a single bite. I prepared his plate and even sliced the meat into little bite-sized pieces. I even offered to spoon-feed him, but he just wouldn't take a single bite.

I got frustrated and angry, so I called my cousins and asked if I could hang out with them. When they said I could, I immediately left with my dad still not having anything for dinner.

When I got back around two in the morning, I thought to check on him and see if he was hungry but decided against it because I was still upset with him and thought that maybe this would teach him a lesson.

He died a few hours later, either on his way to or back from the kitchen. My uncle found him lying unconscious by the kitchen entrance. He probably tried to get something to eat or drink in the middle of the night and had a heart attack or fell over and hit his head. We weren't sure exactly which might have caused his passing, but it didn't matter. My dad was gone, and he died with me being upset with him. I never got the chance to apologize for my impatience. My last moments with him were spent arguing over stupid food. I should have just let him be, or at the very least, I should have checked on him when I got home from my cousin's.

Thinking about the past isn't always a bad thing. Our memories of past mistakes and heartaches have allowed us to survive and become stronger, and hopefully, wiser than we were before. Looking at the past with a different perspective than what we had at the time helps us to heal and move on from the pain that was caused. It also helps us to learn more about ourselves when we apply deeper insight into events that happened.

Why We Should Focus On The Present

It's always good to learn from past mistakes and things that you regret, but when you've been unnecessarily dwelling on the past and wasting your time instead of focusing on solving your current problems and trying to improve your life, it's a problem that you need to solve right away before it drags you down and slows your growth as a person.

Stop dwelling in the past. While there are answers that you can learn from looking back, it's not worth it to keep looking back when you have a whole life ahead of you. There is a big difference between a healthy trip down memory lane and reliving each moment of a terrible experience. One obviously helps, while the other only gets you down. As they say, shit happens, and there is nothing that we can do to change the past, no matter how hard we try. Keep your mind in the here and now so that you do not waste time worrying about things that cannot be changed.

The healthy way to look at these memories is to assess what can be done now to prevent yourself from making the same mistakes or terrible choices you may have made in the past. Everything in life is a lesson, and until that lesson is learned, you are bound to repeat the same mistakes. If you've made many mistakes you regret, or if you've lost so much that looking back only gives you pain, then why dwell on them?

Instead of thinking about the terrible things in your past and making yourself miserable, how about trying to build a better future for yourself instead? It certainly is a better use of your time and energy to work on improving yourself and building a better future.

When you are engrossed in the events of the past, time passes by without you realizing it. What is there to gain in dwelling in your past? Yes, maybe a few wonderful memories. But you could have spent that time on a personal project that you have been putting off or you could have gone to see a new friend and make new memories.

Moving from the Past to the Present

Again, there is nothing wrong with remembering past events. Besides, it is because of those experiences that you are the person that you are today. However, your time is a precious commodity, and you never know when it will come to an end. So take the opportunity to make the most of every moment that you have. Your time is limited, so you have to make sure that you enjoy each moment. Strive to improve yourself and enrich the lives of those around you. That's what I believe is the secret to making life worthwhile.

If you're interested in learning something new, you can take up a class or find a workshop where you can learn something new and useful. If that doesn't work for you, then maybe you can instead find yourself a hobby, one that will keep you productive and happy. There are always new opportunities or directions you can go in your life if you are open and ready when they come. If your attention is in the past, you might miss a good opportunity because you've been looking at the wrong thing. Being grateful for what you have in your life now and working towards personal goals is a better approach.

That should be a better use of your time and energy, right?

Instead of living a life full of regrets, start a bucket list and cross each item off every chance you get. Go and spend time with your family and friends. Keep moving forward with your life. This is the best way to move past regrets that you may hold in your mind and heart.

CHAPTER 4

Master Your Emotions and Express Your Feelings Constructively

I've always been an emotional person. I've said so many hurtful things in my anger, and I've made a lot of poor decisions based on strong emotions. This is what happens when you allow your emotions to rule over your life.

I was nineteen when I met the mother of my daughter. I was so in love with her back then that I didn't want to be away from her for even a minute, so I decided to stop going to school and shacked up with her at her parents' house.

I could have still gone to school; nobody told me to stop going. I could have gone home and just visited her every day after school, but I decided to just stay with her and never leave again. I could have practiced safe sex, but I didn't. I had this naive idea that love is all we needed. We were both very young, and we had our whole lives ahead of us. There was no need to rush into a family, but we did anyway because it "felt right" at the time.

While I won't ever regret having my daughter with my ex, looking back now, we could have done things differently if we'd used our heads even a little more and kept our emotions in check. We were too young and naive, and we didn't have any control over our emotions. We let our emotions control us, and it changed the course of our lives at such a young age.

There were also times when I did shameful things in my anger or frustration, like all those times I tried to kill myself over fights with my ex. Yes, I was in a toxic relationship, and I admit that I was the toxic one.

I've been very selfish. I've tried to commit suicide a few times over things that to me, as an adult looking back, were very shallow and stupid. The closest I got to successfully killing myself was when I jumped off an antenna tower and into my grandma's roof. If I'd fallen into where the frames were, I would have died. Luckily, I hit the gaps and lived.

At the time, offing myself was what felt right because I felt really hurt. The funny thing about it is that the fight probably started over something unimportant because I don't even remember what it was about. I was very selfish. I didn't think about my baby daughter, who could have been orphaned. I didn't think of my parents, who would have lost their only child. I didn't think of my ex, who could have been left feeling guilt that she didn't deserve.

There's nothing I can change about my past, but I've learned to be in control of my emotions a lot better than I used to be. I guess it's mostly because I acknowledge how prone I can be to making poor choices if I let my heart make the decisions for me.

When Emotions Are in Control

Because human beings experience a whole range of emotions, it is very important that we have a handle on our feelings. When you allow your emotions to control you and your actions, there can be a lot of undesired results.

When you allow yourself to react to situations based on your raw emotions and without thinking about what you're about to do, you are setting yourself up to be a slave to your emotions. You may become prone to making mistakes that you could have easily avoided. In the heat of the moment, you might say words or take actions which will bring you to regret once you calm down and come to your senses.

It's okay to "follow your heart" sometimes, as long as you are still fully aware of the consequences of your decisions and that you are willing to live with those consequences. However, you have to remember that your emotions are not always real. What feels right at one moment can be logically wrong. Also, it's easy to make terrible decisions when you're angry or become overly generous and give more than you could afford when you're happy – either way, you might end up in regret. Strong emotions could cloud your judgment, and you may not be able to see the bigger picture. You could be making decisions with just a fraction of the information required to make a sound judgment on matters.

How to Take Back Control of Your Emotions

When you get surprised and start feeling a heavy surge of emotions, try to tell yourself that you need to calm down first instead of actually following through with whatever you're feeling like doing in the heat of the moment. Usually focusing on your breathing or counting in your head should help you calm down even just a little.

Also, try choosing the situations you put yourself in as much as you can. You do not want to put yourself in places, situations or around people which you already know could cause you to have your unwanted emotions triggered.

Try to make a list of your common triggers. These are things that make you automatically lash out in emotion, rather than thinking things through. It may be a certain person or political situation or a particular word or action. That way, you can gain awareness of your triggers which you can then start working on.

If it is a certain person or place, you can try to avoid being around these people or places. If you do not like being rushed, for example, leave ten or fifteen minutes earlier than you are accustomed to so that you do not feel like you are going to be late and you avoid getting upset.

Keep your focus on yourself and your own achievements rather than comparing yourself to other people's assumed accomplishments; it will save you from negative feelings such as envy or jealousy. Remember, you are your own worst enemy. If you think that the people around you are doing better than you, you may become harder on yourself. Be proud of your personal achievements, no matter how small they seem. You are currently a work in progress, and this is something you should never fault yourself for.

A Hard Look at Your Emotional Triggers

There are a few methods you can follow to practice controlling your reactions to stressful events. The most common one is to start taking deep breaths to help calm down your body. This practice will not only keep you from saying things that you might regret, but it will also lower your heart rate and release the tension of your muscles. It can take up to five minutes of taking deep breaths to get your body back to a calm state. While you are breathing, it could also be helpful to try to think happy thoughts or to imagine yourself in a calm relaxing place if you can.

Take a look at your list of emotional triggers and make an effort to work on them. The list can show you instances where you may realize that it's something small that you don't have to get so worked up about.

Once you have mastered not reacting and lashing out with your emotions, you will need to find an outlet that allows you to release these pent-up emotions so that they do not get bottled up. Everyone is different, but some good examples are to talk to someone who can be objective about your feelings or writing them out on paper or a journal. You can also try going to the gym or learning martial arts. Some people find that physical exertion such as weightlifting or practicing martial arts helps to release their emotions. Alternatively, you can go the more passive route and do chanting or meditating to bring you back to your center. Choose a method that resonates with you, and it will help you to control your intense emotions should they arise.

CHAPTER 5

Be the Real You

Back when I was younger, I wanted people to like me. I wanted friends and relationships, so I went all out to give people what I thought they wanted from me. My attitude depended on who I was with and how much I wanted them to like me. I didn't have any loyalties. My opinions shifted depending on the opinions of whoever I was with at the moment. I agreed to everything and never said "no." If it was something I couldn't afford to give, I made every effort to appease and offer something else. In short, I was fake.

I've spent most of my young life being something other than myself. I was a classic people-pleaser. I simply did what I thought would make other people like me.

It is in our nature to want to be accepted, and many people will go to great lengths to ensure they are liked by others. Generally, we try to put our best face forward, which is a mix of qualities and characteristics that we value and wish to be true about ourselves; however, too much of it could make us lose ourselves in the process.

Why Do We Feel The Need to Hide Our True Selves?

One of the main reasons people try to hide their true selves and pretend to be an idealized form of themselves is because they do not want other people to see the negative characteristics they possess.

What we often seem to forget is that there is no such thing as a perfect person out there. It's natural to want to put our best foot forward to make a good first impression, and it's perfectly fine. However, your true nature and flaws will start to show the longer you are in contact with others.

You may "fake it until you make it," pretending to already know or possess something that you want or need in order to project confidence. While there can be a few good aspects to this method such as building confidence, most people use it for the wrong intentions or lose sight of why they fake it in the first place.

Sometimes, when you are not your authentic self, other people can sense it on a subtle level. Because you are not authentic, it could result in people not being able to connect with you on a deeper level. It's also possible to lose yourself in the process of being fake, especially if you've been doing it for a long time.

People who usually feel the need to hide their true selves and bring out a fake persona likely suffer from some sort of self-image or self-esteem issues. They want to be better or at least appear better than what or how they really are because they are seeking attention and approval that they believe they won't get if their real selves are exposed.

Being Authentic Is Key

One day back in college, I started getting text messages from an unknown number. These days, I wouldn't bother with anyone texting or calling me from an unknown number, but back then, in my loneliness, that anonymous person was a welcome friend.

The person seemed to know my thoughts and understand how I felt and shared their own experiences that were somewhat similar to mine. We texted daily for a few weeks, sharing our thoughts and experiences. Apparently, I left my journal one day in class, and she happened to come across it and read it. Then, she got my number from another classmate and decided to text me because she felt the same things I described in my journal.

I will admit that if she didn't hint that she was a girl, I probably wouldn't have entertained her for more than a couple of days. Aside from it feeling creepy, guys aren't supposed to be reading other guys' journal and texting them anonymously. It was sad because I was so lonely at the time that I thought that maybe this anonymous girl could become someone I could have a relationship with because I was desperate to find someone who understood me.

I was so desperate for company that I entertained someone who could have been a stalker. I knew there were potential dangers, but I was desperate. Besides, I knew she was just one of the fifty-or-so females I shared classes with, so what was the harm?

She told me how she just recently got out of an abusive relationship, how she felt used and abused by her ex-boyfriend, and how she felt dirty like she didn't deserve to be loved.

From the way she structured her texts and how she helped me out with homework, I figured that she was very smart. When she finally admitted who she really was, I was very surprised. I had a few classmates I suspected to be her, but I could not have been more wrong. I thought she was one of those quiet girls who rarely spoke in class, but I was very wrong because she turned out to be one of the cute, outgoing ones.

While she wasn't the type who would win beauty pageants, she was not bad-looking either. She had her own group of friends who she always hung out with, and she didn't appear to be someone who had the issues she told me about in her texts. Honestly, I didn't understand why or how different she was in person from her texts.

Because of her, I began to realize that it wasn't about what you are on the surface. Again, this was a person who wasn't ugly, who was nice and likable and highly intelligent. It only goes to show that you can be attractive and be able to communicate well with others, but if you don't see yourself as someone who deserves to be loved, no amount of company will make you feel happy and contented.

It's really not about being attractive and fashionable. It's not even about having a lot of people you call friends. You can be the most awesome person in the world and never realize it because you don't see your own value.

It got me thinking some more. Honestly, I was tired of feeling like I was always chasing after people. I was tired of acting cool. I decided to just be me and that I wouldn't care how others saw me or what they thought about me. I was done trying to do things for people who didn't make me feel appreciated.

When I made this change in my thinking, that's when the magic started to happen. As soon as I stopped worrying too much about how I should act so that everyone would like me, I must have changed on the outside in some way that I didn't notice myself, because little by little, I started making friends. What surprised me was that these friends that I made didn't care about how I was. I could be rude, I could make mistakes, I could tell them "no," and they wouldn't become hostile.

It felt great. I never thought that I could even have friends who liked me for just me. I didn't realize until then how good it felt, or that it was even possible to have people who really like me even when I don't give them anything or when I disagree with them.

I'll admit, I don't have hundreds of friends. I also have been turned down and friend-zoned by women, and I am by no means a pickup artist. But, the handful of friends I have are real friends that I'll be more than happy to go through the thick or thin with, and I am a hundred percent sure that they also feel the same for me. I also have a girlfriend who loves me even if I make dumb jokes and thinks I'm sexy even if I'm obese. All my relationships are real. I'm real to people in my life, and all of them are real to me. I don't spend any time, money, or extra effort in trying to please people in my life so they will keep being in my life. Everyone I have in my life takes me just as I am, as I take them just as they are. I am happy and content with myself and my relationships, and the things I feel discontentment about are more of the monetary kind. Of course, I wish I was a lot wealthier with mansions all over the world and driving around in six-figure luxury cars, but loneliness and emptiness are not problems for me because I know that I will always have someone, and if no one is available, I always have myself.

Why You Need to Be Real

Pretending to be something or someone else is not going to get you any real connections and relationships. If people like you for the fake you, then what happens if you slip up and show your true self? Would they still like you or would they suddenly find you repulsive and go away?

Isn't it exhausting to keep having to be conscious of your every word and action? I know it is because I did it for a very long time. I just kept on adjusting and giving in to other people. Often, I would find that nothing I do is ever enough because people seem to just always want more and more from me. I always had to observe and think of how to keep people happy with me.

If you haven't figured it out, let me be the one to tell you that it's simply not possible to please everybody. There are probably people in your life that you're simply not comfortable with for reasons that you yourself aren't sure of. Maybe you just can't figure them out, or maybe there's something about the way they talk. It's the same for other people. There would always be people who simply won't be fond of you for certain reasons. Maybe it's even the fact that they can sense that you're not real with them that throws them off.

In any case, if what you really want is to make real, meaningful relationships, you have to put yourself out there and show people the real you. The ones who learn to like you and appreciate the real you are the ones who are going to stick around for a long time and the people who don't like the real you usually aren't worth your company anyway.

Whoever you may be and whatever flaws you are worried about, there's always something good about you that you can offer. You're an awesome person; you just have to really make an effort to look at all the good things about you and learn to appreciate yourself a little more. There would always be people out there who can learn to love and appreciate you for who and what you really are; it just takes patience.

CHAPTER 6

Building Confidence

Confidence is an attribute that all humans need in order to function socially. For some people, it comes naturally while for some, it takes some work to build.

I used to think that confidence and attractiveness were directly correlated. The more attractive you are, the more confidence you have. But from what I learned from the people I've known over the years, it seems that it's the other way around – the more confident you are, the more attractive you become.

A good example of this is a guy we'll call Ed who I was familiar with back in college. Excuse me for objectifying here, but that guy wasn't someone you'd call attractive, but he had all these pretty girlfriends who he seems to keep replacing with another attractive girlfriend every few weeks. Seriously, that guy was something else. I got to befriend one of his exes who told me that there was something about the way he walked and talked that made him attractive.

It helped me realize that confidence and physical attractiveness aren't related at all. You can be the most attractive person in the world, but if you lack confidence, you wouldn't be able to see it and appreciate it even if you're looking at yourself directly in a mirror. On the other hand, you can be an average-looking person but feel attractive because you have a lot of self-confidence.

Your Inner Voice and Thought Patterns

Sometimes our inner voice can be our harshest critic. Have you ever noticed that you are constantly putting yourself down? Does your inner voice always seem to tell you negative things about yourself? Do you always find yourself worrying about things going wrong? If so, it is time to take control. You have to start questioning your negative inner self and challenge what it is saying.

Try to be aware of your thoughts. When you start noticing that the things that you're worried about are no longer making sense, try focusing your thoughts on something else, preferably something positive and productive. If you find yourself dwelling on the things that could go wrong, try refocusing your thoughts on problem-solving.

Learn to accept that you're only human. It's impossible for you to know everything. It's impossible for you to control everything. It's also impossible for you to predict the future so stop worrying about the things you can't do anything about. Do yourself a favor and try to go easy on yourself.

I want you to learn to look at the things you're worried about and try to see if you currently have the power to fix them. Is worrying going to help you fix things? Is all this worrying accomplishing anything, or are you feeling like you are just running in circles?

If it's something that you have the power to do something about right now, then why not do something about it instead of wasting your time and energy worrying?

If it's something you can't do anything about at the moment, what do you need to fix the problem? What steps can you take to stop worrying so much and focus on the here and now?

If it's something that you absolutely cannot do anything about, is there any point in even thinking about it? Perhaps it is best to shift your thinking to something more positive or an issue that can actually be handled in a constructive way.

I know, it's not as easy as I make it sound, but do try to shift your focus as a favor to yourself. Just worrying is not going to help you fix anything. Perhaps, it's time you took on a more problem-solving oriented approach.

Different Methods to Gain Self-Confidence

An effective method in building your confidence is to try to get out of your comfort zone by doing something that scares you each day. Of course, don't go all-in on the first day. Do baby steps. Think small yet consistent. This could be as simple as taking another route to work or just greeting someone at work.

Additionally, you can try to take small personal challenges each day that could give you quick and easy wins just to get yourself a little boost. Then, work on gradually increasing the difficulty of these challenges. The bottom line is to push the envelope and conquer your daily challenge. Every time that you are successful, you strengthen your confidence levels. Eventually, you can be able to face your fears head-on.

Remember that when you are setting personal goals for yourself, do not shoot for the moon right away. You might only end up setting yourself up for failure if you give yourself too much too soon. However, if you start with smaller and more achievable goals, you will build your confidence more quickly. If you find that you are consistently crossing off your goals from your list, you can start to make more challenging goals for yourself. Little by little, you will accomplish everything that you set out to do, and you will continue to push yourself to achieve more.

If you are interested in a more structured challenge, try the rejection challenge for three months. This concept comes from Jia Jiang, who is the author of the book Rejection Proof. He received rejections of differing levels from different people over the course of 100 days. The purpose was to desensitize himself from the feeling of being rejected, which helped him to overcome his fears much more swiftly. I haven't tried it myself, but it certainly seems interesting.

Another proven way to deal with fear was written about by Ronald Siegel, who was a Harvard Medical School professor. In his book titled The Mindfulness Solution, he suggests that you ponder about your worst fear for a significant amount of time in order to understand it. Think about the worst-case scenario that can occur and focus on your breathing patterns. Basically, it's like putting yourself in a simulation. It's also supposed to desensitize you from your worst fears.

It is also helpful to keep a list of the goals that you have achieved. This will be a reminder of the struggles you may have had in the past which you have overcome. It will also be a reminder of your track record of continuing to push towards more challenging goals. When you have proof that you are capable of overcoming difficult obstacles, you will have less fear when you start to set your new goals.

Another helpful method is to get out of yourself and help others. When you work with people who are in need of help, it will remind you to be grateful for the things that you have. This exercise will aid you in recognizing your strengths, especially if you use your knowledge to help others. Not only will you feel good about helping other people, but you will also build your confidence in the process.

You can also practice positive affirmations. These are statements that lift the spirit and are ideas that we can tell ourselves in order to build our confidence. They are more effective when they are said aloud and can be made into a type of mantra which is said each day.

When you are trying to improve your self-confidence, you need to take a long, hard look at yourself and figure out where you need to improve. It could help to start a journal where you can record the thoughts you have about yourself. If you find that you have many negative thoughts about yourself, you will need to start analyzing the reasons behind these thoughts and try to challenge them to see whether they are true or not.

Next, you will need to take a look at your limitations and why you have them in the first place. Again, you become your own worst enemy when it comes to realizing your full potential whenever you listen to your negative inner voice. When you start to remove these limiting and negative thoughts from your mind, you will allow yourself to go after whatever personal goals you set out for yourself.

Another way to start building confidence in yourself is to put some effort into your personal appearance. This can be as simple as smiling more or caring more about your posture. These are little things that can start a chain reaction leading to a major change in how you feel about yourself.

This idea does not just apply to how you look on the outside because what's on the inside matters just as much, if not more. Besides working on making your thoughts and beliefs more positive, you need to put some energy into practicing gratitude for what you have in life.

The Power of Positive Thinking

Positive thinking is an excellent tool because you are setting yourself up to focus on good things. When your thoughts are focused on the positive, your actions will start to follow suit. When you do your best to act in a positive way consistently, even in difficult situations, you are more likely to get positive results.

It can also be helpful to say encouraging words to yourself. This is sometimes referred to as self-affirmation and can be very effective even during highly stressful times and situations. If you are able to give yourself pep-talks, it could greatly increase your self-confidence levels.

For every negative thought that you have about yourself, challenge yourself to discover five positive thoughts. Take at least half a minute to think about each of the positive thoughts to train your brain. This should be effective in bringing about more positive thoughts during the day.

If you are having trouble finding something to be grateful for in your life, take a deep breath. You are still reading this, right? Then you have a big reason to be grateful. You can read. Also, you can afford to buy a book to help you with your issues. There are people in the world who don't know how to read or write, and there are people who can't even imagine buying books because they can barely afford to buy food. When can switch your perspective to notice things that you may take for granted, you will find a lot of things in your life to be grateful for. This should also help you build confidence.

Take the time to sit down and write a list of all the things, big and small, that you are grateful for. When you have completed this task, write a separate list of all the of the accomplishments you are proud of. When complete, post these lists somewhere you will always see them so you that you can just look at them anytime and feel good about yourself.

CHAPTER 7

Setting Boundaries and Learning To Say No

If you've ever hung out with a toddler before, you'll hear the word "no" a lot. As Bunmi Laditan cleverly titled her book, Toddlers Are Assholes and it's because whatever you offer or ask them to do, the answer you'll get out of them is very likely to be "no."

Why is it so easy for them to say no? According to some theories on child development, children in the toddler stage have just come to realize that they are separate and independent from their caregivers. It's like they just discovered that they have superpowers, so they try to exercise and test these new-found powers.

As they grow up, some children start to learn that "no" can be a dirty word because their caregivers or their peers seem to get upset with them whenever they express their refusal, and they begin to associate refusal to cooperate with feelings of guilt. And, because guilt can be such an uncomfortable feeling, some of them eventually decide that they would rather agree to things that they don't really want to do or give things that they don't really want to give than feel guilty when they refuse.

I've been struggling with feelings of guilt when I tell someone "no" ever since I can remember. I remember how some of my friends would stop playing with me if I didn't get them the snacks they wanted, and it made me feel heavy inside because I know that they were upset with me.

It's been so ingrained in me that even until now, I still feel heavy inside whenever I have to tell someone "no," but I also know that I have to put my own needs first and I respect myself enough to know not to give any more than I'm willing to give.

Defining Your Boundaries

Saying no to somebody can sometimes take a lot more effort and can be a lot more complicated, especially when it is someone of authority like your boss when they are asking you to do something that's beyond your job description. However, there are many ways that you can refuse and set firm boundaries without feeling guilty and without getting the other person upset.

First, you have to learn to respect yourself and understand that you are not responsible for other people's problems, and you are not required to give them anything that you're not willing to give. This is, of course, assuming that the other people we're referring to aren't your kids or anyone you're legally or professionally responsible for.

Next, you have to be firm and unrelenting in your refusal. You have to resist the urge to give in no matter what and not even once because that's how other people learn to acknowledge your limits and respect your boundaries. Always remember that what you allow is what will continue.

Make it clear what you are willing and not willing to do from the beginning and stand by it. That's how you gain respect.

Even if you have set boundaries, there will still be people who will try to test those boundaries. I know that it can get really annoying when someone keeps on pestering you with the same request over and over. But, it doesn't give you the excuse to be rude. There are ways for you to refuse without being rude or offending people and that's what we'll be discussing next.

The Art of Saying No

In most cases, you actually do not have to say the word "no." You just have to say "yes" a little less often. What I mean is that you have to be more aware and be more careful of the things that you agree to.

If you are in the habit of automatically saying "yes" to any request that is asked of you, then this applies to you perfectly. Being a yes-person may have allowed you to avoid a lot of conflict in the past, but you probably also got left feeling used or abused.

If the word "no" rarely comes out of your mouth, you can start the process now by not agreeing to any non-important, non-urgent request for the next 24 hours. Just tell anyone asking you a favor that you'll think about it and that you will get back to them tomorrow. This should give you the time to really think things over and see if it's something you really want to give or not. It also gives you time to come up with a polite way to refuse should that be what you decide to do.

Continue the process of giving things time before you agree and change your default answer from "yes" into "hold on" or "I'll think about it" then try not to give the other person a chance to convince you to give an immediate answer by telling them that you'll talk about it again once you've had the chance to think.

If the idea of confrontation is still too difficult as you become too nervous and will still respond with a "yes," try to write out your response. This can be through a text message, email, or written letter. It gives you more control, and you will have the opportunity to say exactly what you want to say without forgetting any details, which may happen when you're under the pressure of a face to face situation.

Remember that when you are telling someone "no," there is no need to be mean and aggressive. You are exercising your personal boundaries, and it is within your rights as a person but remember that other people have feelings too. You simply need to say that it is not going to work out. You can also add that you will get back to them once you're in a better situation to help them out. You will find that keeping it simple usually works out best. Just keep any responses lighthearted and be honest about your reasons. They do not need to hear a long story about your life that makes you unable to grant their request.

If you start feeling guilty, keep in mind that when you tell anyone "no," this is not necessarily a reflection of how you feel about this person or what they really mean to you. It's rarely personal as sometimes things just cannot work with your current situation.

Sometimes, instead of a flat out refusal, you can help the person making a request to find an alternative solution or maybe point them in the direction of someone else who may be able to help them.

Do not beat around the bush and just say what you feel in a polite manner. If you do not want to do the favor, say "no." A common mistake, other than saying "yes" to something you do not want to do, is indulging the need to explain your reason for rejecting the request fully.

Of course, it is your choice to tell the person the "why," but it should be kept short and should not be a long dialogue about everything that has gone wrong with your life.

There are times when you have to make long explanations, but if it's not something that you absolutely have to do, then it's always best to keep your refusals short and polite.

The more you say "no" to requests that you don't agree with, the easier it gets over time. You will start to take back control of your life, giving yourself the time that you need to perform your own tasks and save your resources for yourself. You have to remember to take care of yourself first before you start worrying about others. Putting yourself first should eventually place you in a better position to help other people.

It's not always easy to assert your own needs, to speak honestly about what you want or don't want, and to put your needs in front of others. You may think that you are not a good person when you tell someone you care about that you are not able to do something for them. But, you also have to believe that if these people really care about you, they should also be able to understand your situation and accept your refusal.

CHAPTER 8

Improve Your Social Skills

If you ever get worried about the way you talk or whether you would be able to understand or relate to other people, I want you to remember my dad. This is how awesome my dad was. The greatest communicator I have ever seen.

He was deaf and mute, which by default made him unable to speak or listen to anyone. Yes, you read that right. HE CANNOT HEAR, AND HE CANNOT SPEAK. But, that guy had A LOT of friends.

If you go to the town where I grew up in and ask someone who "umel"(the native word for mute) is, they would either tell you they're friends with him or at least point you to someone who is his friend.

As a kid, growing up with a disabled parent is not a good experience. I always got teased for having a deaf-mute dad, and some kids even made fun of him, and it upset me a lot.

I felt ashamed to have him as my dad when I was a little kid. But, as I grew up, I learned to admire him.

My dad had great confidence and social skills despite his particular disabilities. Whenever he was in some new place, he would randomly approach someone and strike up a "conversation." Give him ten minutes in any random social situation, and you'll find him laughing with a circle of men around him.

I know a lot of people without any disadvantages who don't have a tenth of the number of friends my dad had.

There have been a lot of instances where I've gotten free stuff, or I've been done a good favor just for being his son.

In the Philippines, each town has an annual feast date. There would be a huge flea market where they would sell a lot of interesting stuff from clothes to pillows to even fireworks. Usually, there would also be a carnival with many different rides, and the spot where they put up the carnival will be closed off with these temporary walls and in order to get in an enjoy the games and the rides, you would either have to pay the entrance fee at the gate which steadily increased every day, reaching its peak at the feast night, or find a way to jump over a ten-feet-high wall.

When I was a kid, I never had to pay entrance fees because my dad was friends with all the cops watching by the gate, and he would also make quick friends with the actual carnival people who ran the whole operation. That also meant that I also got to ride everything for free, and on occasion, I was also allowed to play a few games at no cost.

One time, I also got to hang out with the guys who ran the snake show. It was then that I found out that they took off the fangs of the cobras they kept, which also meant that this guy whose name was supposed to be Zuma wasn't really immune to snake poison. It's just that the snakes had no fangs to inject him with poison in the first place. Also, his name wasn't really Zuma, he wasn't the king of anything, and he was just a regular guy who ate regular food and watched TV when he wasn't on stage. Never meet your heroes.

My dad has been a great example for me as he has shown me over and over that there's nothing wrong with approaching random people and try to strike a conversation.

I learned early in life that people were generally approachable, and most were willing to talk to you if you engage them in meaningful conversations. I mean my dad was deaf and mute! If he can do it, then there's no excuse in my mind for anyone who can hear and talk not to approach someone else and talk to them.

Just to be clear here, just because I have enough confidence to approach and talk to anyone, doesn't mean that I don't worry about what other people think of me. Also, unlike my dad, I don't just randomly approach someone and start talking to them. I still believe that my dad was just one of the really special ones who had talent. That was his superpower, and if he wasn't deaf or mute, he would probably be president.

"No man is an island," it is said, and human beings have to rely on other people for their needs and to have a fulfilling life. We build relationships of different kinds because we recognize that we need to connect with other people in order to be successful, and the basis of all successful relationships is effective communication.

Effective communication skills are mandatory for anyone who wants to be successful and happy.

While it's common knowledge that the more articulate you are with your words, the better you are at communicating with others, what many people don't understand is that words by themselves aren't the only things that a person needs in order to be successful at communicating with others. Things like body language - gestures, posture and facial expressions, the tone of our voices, our accents, the way we make our entrance and the way we leave the conversation, as well as the way we structure our sentences all have a significant impact on how effective we are in relaying our message and making an impact to others.

My quick guide on how to make a great first impression and start meaningful conversations should help you with that, especially if you are worried about how to start. You can get it for free from my website at https://johnfernando.com.

The Art of Listening and Paying Attention

It's funny how conversations happen with my dad. The moment my dad approaches someone, a process happens:

First, my dad gets the persons attention by mildly poking them on the shoulder and smiling at them. The person looks at him, surprised.

Next, my dad starts doing sign language, points at something funny and laughs. At this point, the person then switches from surprised, to confused.

After a few seconds, my dad, looking at the person and gauging their reaction, either tries to slow down and repeats what he just did, or tries a different set of signs and gestures but always finishes with the funny laugh.

After a few tries, the person switches from confused, to "oh, I get it!" and he laughs along with my dad.

Then, my dad has them. The person will either try their best to do their own sign language with my dad carefully and cheerfully observing what they try to say and how their facial expressions are, then he comes up with some sign language joke, and they laugh again.

This happens for a while depending on whatever arbitrary thing that my dad decides but moments later, he and that person will be shaking hands, both smiling, and he either tells the guy to come with him and approach us to introduce his new friend with the guy shyly introducing himself, or they pat each other in the shoulder, part ways with both of them still smiling.

The next time he approaches the person, he smiles at him, pats him on the shoulder, and proudly tells anyone close enough to see him do his signs that this guy is his good friend. My dad never forgets anyone he has ever had a conversation with. Next thing me and my mom know, he's asking the guy a favor, and the guy is more than happy to accommodate my dad's request, and my mom feels embarrassed about my dad asking for favors from another stranger.

I'm telling you, my dad has superpowers. This happens every single time when we go to some random place where we don't know anyone.

I think the key to my dad's success is that he "listens." As in really listens or in his case, observes carefully and attentively. He only has the body language part down, but he is a true master at it.

This is what I think everyone should be doing more: listening and paying attention to what the other person, reading them and trying our best to understand what they are really saying then coming up with a reply that makes both of you happy.

Again, let me stress out the importance of carefully observing and listening to the other person and thinking about how to best respond.

Often, we make the wrong assumption that in order to be great communicators, we simply have to talk clearly so that the other person can hear us.

We forget that talking and relaying our message is only half of the conversation. Sometimes, we even become rude and interrupt the other person, and we try to talk over them because we feel like we are not being heard.

We listen partially and often only pay attention to the keywords that we want to hear and end up losing the full context of the message that the other person is trying to tell us.

Instead, the best approach is to listen to the other person completely and actively until they are finished speaking. Then, take a moment when it is your turn to speak to think about what you are going to say next. Not only will this make the conversation deeper, but you will also become more genuinely connected to the person you are speaking with. Make eye contact with the other person to let them know that you are invested in the words they are speaking. Read their body language to see if they are as engaged as you are in the conversation.

Ask questions to let them know that you are interested in the conversation and that you are curious about knowing more. The result of actively listening is the other person will be more open and honest with their feelings and thoughts because they will feel like they can trust you.

Being a Trustworthy Confidant

Ultimately, you would want to win the trust of other people by being a confidant, which means that they trust you with their secrets and in order to do that, you must be able to prove that you are worth their time, that you can empathize with them, and that you can be trusted.

For example, if someone comes to you with a concern or seeks your advice, try to be objective and understand their position. Try to put yourself in their shoes because in this instance, this other person is looking for a friend or someone to confide something personal in and they thought that you were worthy enough for them to trust with their problems. They are not looking for someone to beat them down or pass judgment. They are looking to you for a little support. Even if you do not agree with everything that they are talking about, you should still listen attentively, hold off judgment, and come up with that you believe is the best response.

With this said, you should understand that there is a fine line to tread when giving people advice. Unless they express that they want your opinion, it is best to keep your thoughts to yourself and simply show them that you are listening to them attentively. Sometimes giving unsolicited advice comes across as passing judgment, which is not going to help the other person.

If you believe that you may be able to help them with your advice, then politely ask the person after they are done talking if you can give your own opinion and if you think that it might offend them even just a little, you may try to soften the blow by also telling them that they might not like what you would say and again confirm with them if they want you to proceed.

Remember that this is not about you, but it's about the other person. Out of all the people that this person has in their life, they decided that you were the best one to turn to regarding this particular issue so you should consider it an honor. I know that sometimes it's a bother to listen to other people's problems, but you also have to consider this person's feelings.

Also, remember to keep your conversations confidential. It's their life and their issues. It is not for you to share with other people unless they explicitly tell you to do so.

Now I know that being a confidant is going to take time, and we are supposed to be talking about social skills here.

But the fact of the matter is that the principles I have told you about being a confidant are exactly what you need in order to be more successful socially.

You have to be able to project that you're listening attentively to the other person. You have to try your best to put yourself in the other person's shoes and try to see things in their perspective. Also, you have to remember that people are not looking to be judged or looked down on, so you have to be courteous in the way you speak and show respect. You should also do your best not to be judgemental and only talk once you've listened fully and have thought of the best possible reply.

In order to improve your social skills, the best skill you need to develop is actually not in how you talk or act. Instead, it's listening and paying attention to everything that other people are saying and not just their words, but the nonverbal parts of communication. Pay attention, observe for cues, and always think about your response.

CHAPTER 9

Building Meaningful Relationships

There used to be a time when I would go on social media and look up people from my past - ex-girlfriends, old friends, and a few acquaintances. I would check their profiles and see what they were up to.

I know, stalker alert. In my defense, I didn't go looking through years of posts or pictures. I would just take a quick look to see how they were doing.

My thing was thinking about all the times I've had with these people, the good and the bad.

Sometimes, it was about the women I should have asked out when I had the chance but didn't because I didn't have enough courage at the time. I would try to imagine how my life would have been if I'd actually just gathered up my courage and asked them out.

For a few old friends, I would think about all the fun we all had together and wish that I could go back to those times, which should have lasted forever. For some of them, I actually tried to reconnect, and we hit it off like no time had passed since, but for some, I found out that we'd become very different people whose time together had long since expired.

It's great to have friends and to be in a romantic relationship. Being with the right people can make your life more colorful, and I consider myself very lucky to have found real friends who have made even the simplest of things feel fun and interesting.

I also consider myself honored by having the privilege of being with the different women I have been with throughout my life. There were good and bad moments. Most of them ended badly, but I still appreciate having the opportunity to learn from each relationship.

There was even this ex-girlfriend who would get upset if I forgot something, said something in a different way, or even if I listened to songs with a certain message. She would always find things to get jealous or upset about. For example, just letting the song "Sad to Belong" by England Dan and John Ford Coley finish playing on the radio one time caused her to get upset because according to her, I'm probably into someone else and regretting being with her because I let the song play out. It wasn't even my radio! Was I supposed to cover my ears!?

It may surprise you to know that the relationship lasted over a year. Now, I'm not saying I wasn't without my faults, but seriously, I got that she loved me and she was afraid of losing me. I knew that she really cared about me, and that's the reason I stayed that long. I guess at the time, I was also afraid that nobody else would love me as intensely as she did.

I understand very well how hard it could be for some people to connect with other people, either to make friends with them or to get into romantic relationships. That's probably one of the reasons that you got my book because you felt like you needed help.

If you've been paying attention to my stories, you'll know that there used to be a time when I didn't have any real friends.

A lot of the friends I had were people who just wanted to get something out of me, and I was full of insecurities and self-doubt.

I spent a lot of sleepless nights thinking about why I wasn't happy and wondering what I might have been doing wrong. I made sure that I gave my best to please my friends, but for some reason, I still felt lonely and unappreciated.

I hope that at this point, you've at least realized the need for you to love yourself, overcome your fears, and be authentic.

Keep in mind that not everyone will like you and appreciate you no matter what you do and that's okay.

I also want you to understand that sometimes, the people you want in your life may not be the best people for you.

You must have at least one specific person in mind that you want to be friends with or that you want to attract and be in a romantic relationship with. Unfortunately, this is not the book that will teach you that, or at least this is not a book that will teach you how to manipulate them into liking you. Rather, this is a book that will show you how to approach them, make a connection, and if you hit it off - how you can keep them with you for as long as they'll want to stay. I hope I didn't mislead you in any way in thinking that this book was going to teach you some secret mind techniques in order to convince a particular person to like you or fall in love with you and be with you forever.

The only real person that I specifically want you to be friends with and love with all your heart is none other than yourself. Do that, and you'll be able to find the right people to come into your life and make it colorful.

It may not be the people you initially wanted, but often, you'll find that these people who will come into your life once you learn to be yourself are much better than those people you idealized.

However, in the interest of helping you maintain great-quality relationships, I'm going to give you a secret that I've discovered for myself along the way, and it's this:

Relationships of every kind require a form of give and take. Generally, the ones that succeed and last for a long time are the ones that have a healthy balance where the amount given is about the same as the amount received. If I'm making it sound like a business transaction, it's because, in a way, it is.

When you buy something, you generally agree that the money you're paying is equal to the value of the thing you're getting. When you think that you overpaid for it, you start feeling that you've been ripped off and you get upset. If, on the other hand, you think that you got it at a bargain, you feel happy about it.

Also, much like business and trade, scarcity and abundance play a factor in determining someone's value. In business, usually, when there's a lot of something, it's value goes down. When this something suddenly becomes scarce, the value goes up.

In relationships, be it friendly or the romantic type, we're sort of buying from each other, although the currency is the intangible kind, namely love and affection. We give our love and affection to the people we want in our lives in the hopes that they will give us the same.

The more you want someone to be in your life, the more you value them and the further you're willing to go for them.

Now, the problem is when you start giving too much without getting any affection or appreciation in return. Also, as you keep giving and giving, you create an abundance, and your value to the people you keep giving to goes down, and they could end up taking you for granted.

Just to be clear, I'm not saying you can't value someone more than your life. I, myself, value my daughter more than my life. I'm also not saying that giving yourself to people is wrong, nor is trying to please other people. All I'm saying is that you have to be careful and you have to remember still to think about yourself.

Only give what you can afford to really give and make sure that you can still say "no" whenever you want to. The moment you start feeling like you're giving too much, then you probably are. When you start wondering if you should give more than you already have, then you're probably already giving more than enough.

The people who really care about you won't mind if you tell them no, and they won't ask you to give them any more than you're willing to.

Now that you know the secret in maintaining healthy and successful relationships let me share with you what I have learned in terms of finding the right people to be in your life because sometimes, they don't just come out of the blue. Sometimes, you have to be the one to make a move.

How to Make New Friends and Build Lasting Friendships

When you have made a true friend, they are going to stick with you through the thick and thin. They are going to be the ones who are going to cry with you when you cry and laugh along with you when times are great. They will even be there to bail you out of jail if you've made the wrong decision – as long as they are not in there sitting right next to you. So how do you find someone who is worthy of true friendship?

First is to approach people. Find out where the people who will have things in common with you hang out and spend their time. This is important because most relationships are built on the foundation of having something in common.

Of course, when you set your mind to meeting new friends, you are going to need to be dedicated to the idea of going out more than you have been in the past. You are simply not going to meet new people while sitting on your couch every night. Think outside the box as well, and sign up for hobbies you have interest in so that you can find like-minded people to hang out with.

For example, if you're into classical music, your first choice shouldn't probably be attending a rock concert. I mean there's nothing wrong in exploring other genres. You can try, but unless you're intimately familiar with the bands that are going to be playing and know the lyrics to their songs, then you'll find it hard to find something to talk about with another person in that concert. Does that make sense?

Now if you attend a classical music concert then everyone there is a potential person for you to connect with because you share classical music in common. It should be easy for you to strike a conversation and make things interesting because you will be able to quickly and easily relate to the other people there.

Also, you can meet new people through your existing friends or the people who are already in your life like your coworkers. Again, that's another thing in common.

Be sure to accept invitations to social events or to simply hang out and do something as long as they are possible within your schedule. When you are invited, not only will you already know someone who is going, they are likely going to invite other people who you might get the chance to know and befriend. Of course, if you make a habit of making excuses not to come or cancel at the last minute, you are going to be invited to events less and less, until nobody would want to invite you because they'll assume that you'll just refuse or worse, they might think that you don't like them.

Even for those that are not shy, the initial meeting of new people can be stressful, and they don't always hit it off so you shouldn't worry about not hitting it off with anyone right at the beginning. Just focus on attending and being your best authentic self. You never know what is in store, but this is part of socializing. It can go a myriad of ways. Just be open to new experiences and use it as an opportunity to practice your social and communication skills. Who knows, you might just find someone that you instantly connect with and be friends with them for a very long time.

This reminds me of my best friend, Juanita. I got introduced to her through our mutual cousin on a grocery shopping trip. I am from our cousin's father's side while she is from her mother's side. My cousin asked me to go shopping with her, and we picked up Juanita to go shopping with us.

She was very nice, and she did try to talk to me as we were walking through the aisles of the store, but I was still very shy, and I was still adjusting to my new life here in the US back then so I wasn't interested in making friends with her or anyone else just yet.

We passed by the aisle where they had these little plastic trash bins, and I mentioned that I needed one fo those, but I didn't bring my wallet with me at the time, so I wasn't able to get it.

The following week, when I got home from work, there was a new plastic trash bin by my door, and my aunt told me that Juanita dropped it off for me. It was very sweet. She remembered that I wanted a trash bin for my room and she got me one. I added her immediately on facebook and messaged her my thanks, to which she offered to drive me to the store if I ever needed to buy some supplies because I didn't have my driver's license yet at the time.

Then from there, we started shopping together, and she would bring me to her house after we were done shopping and she would make dinner, and I got to hang out with her family. I also became good friends with her kids, who are around my age. I also got to meet my other best friend Jillian who is her daughter.

Back when I needed a new place to stay because my landlady's daughter was coming back home and needed her room back, Juanita and her husband agreed to let me stay with them which lasted for a year.

It was a year of pure fun, and I learned a lot about the American and Mexican cultures from living with them. It was where I learned to enjoy watching Football and became an Oakland Raiders fan because they were all Raider fans.

I owe that woman a lot, and I'm sure that I would have never made it through the last nine years here in the US without her friendship and all the things I learned from her family.

Imagine that. The most beautiful and most meaningful friendship I have ever had in my life started with a small plastic trash bin. Now I wish I kept that trash bin with me when I moved.

That's how I got to meet and have my best friend for nine years, and at the time of writing this book, I have been here for ten. You never know how you'll meet the right people that would make your life wonderful and fun, so never turn down an invitation that could let you meet more people if you want to make more friends.

How to Find the Perfect Romantic Partner

When you are able to find a partner to share your life with, it can bring much more joy in your life. Of course, it is not always easy to find that one person who really fits with you perfectly. Most of the time, people go from relationship-to-relationship until they find the right one who will stick for the rest of their lives. In some rare cases, some partners find each other from a young age and stick together for the rest of their lives without having tried being in a relationship with other people. I personally know a couple of friends who have only been with one person their entire lives, and I think it's awesome for them to have found the one at such an early age and how it all worked out for all those years.

Just like finding new friends, usually, the best place to start is going to places where people you have common interests with hang out and you can also meet them through your friends and acquaintances.

The main difference, however, is that there is the added element of attraction. You do not have to find anything attractive about your friends, but most romantic relationships usually start with some sort of attraction which is usually physical but not always.

My dating and relationship experience has been a good mix between being physically attracted to a woman or being attracted to them because of their intelligence or unique personalities. I try to avoid being shallow and limited by physical appearance because I have always understood that beauty fades.

Sometimes, I become attracted to a beautiful woman only to be turned off by their ugly personalities or lack of intelligence. Sometimes, I become attracted to women who are kind or smart and don't even notice their attractiveness until later.

The key to finding the perfect partner is not just looking at one aspect but in their totality and in how they impact you as a person. It has to be someone who inspires you to be a better person and helps you bring out your best self.

I used to be a romantic and believed that the perfect partner is someone who completes you and fills the missing things in you. But now that I know what I know, I disagree with my old self's assessment.

I don't know if you agree with me on this, but I believe that you should be complete before you even find a partner to spend your life with. I believe that a romantic relationship should be a compliment and not a supplement to your life. I believe that if you are expecting your partner to fill a hole in you or make up for something that you lack, then you're codependent and it's not healthy or fair for the both of you.

I would not spend much time explaining my point because this can get very tricky. Feel free to agree and disagree with me on this, but there are a few things that are universal in building a successful relationship.

First, the ideal partner is someone who is secure within themselves, kind, honest, stable, and cooperative. The people who have these qualities tend to be more mature and have had life experiences which have broadened their horizons.

Even though you may be chomping at the bit to share your life with someone, any relationship worth having in the long-term is going to take time. Also, do not decrease your value by dating someone who does not have the same values as you or that you cannot be yourself around at all times. A good person is going to accept you for everything that you are, flaws and all, and they will also support you in your personal growth.

When you are getting to know the person, you need to be honest and straightforward with them. If you are simply looking for someone to have fun with or somebody to hopefully settle down with one day, let the potential partner know. Of course, do not blurt out on your first date that you are looking to get married. The better way to put it is that you have been on the dating scene for a while, and you are looking for someone more solid and real to spend your time with. I'm of course assuming here that this is what you want.

Everyone has different ideas and goals for being in a relationship, and you want to make sure that you are on the same page from the very beginning. This saves you both from misunderstandings and expectations which were never expressed.

The first few dates can be really exhilarating and exciting! However, try to keep a level of balance between logic and feelings. Of course, everyone loves the feeling of being in love, but it should never be forced. If it is meant to be, your relationship is going to unfold and feel right naturally. Of course, your partner is not going to be perfect, so if you put them on a pedestal early on while you are dating, this could be a problem in the long run.

Be sure to keep up your social life outside of the relationship. You had a life before you met this special person, and it is best to keep up your normal routine and not include them in everything in your life. Not only does this build a healthy relationship, but it will also help you to have experiences to talk about that did not involve them. Just because you're in a relationship doesn't mean that you no longer have a personal life.

I apologize if this is you and if this offends you, but I'm gonna have to say that being in a relationship does not mean requiring your partner to share with you all of their passwords and looking into their text messages and hacking into their social media accounts.

That, to me, is a sign of a toxic relationship. There still has to be a sign of respect, and you have to be able to trust each other completely. For me, the moment that you have doubts about the relationship, then it's the beginning of the end of the relationship.

You have to keep from being too attached to each other, which is not a healthy base for a relationship. Allow your partner to have breathing room and personal time so that they do not feel too overwhelmed with all the changes a relationship ultimately brings.

Another great aspect to look for in a potential partner is a team player who is able to compromise when it is needed. When two people start to blend their lives, ideas, and thoughts, there should be some give and take. Be sure that any give and take is as balanced as possible where neither one of you is taking more than what you are giving. This will ensure that there will not be a dominating person who is controlling the relationship. This is another thing I want to emphasize. A healthy relationship should be egalitarian and not dominated by one partner. You should be able to talk things out and come up with decisions and relationship policies that both of you fully agree with.

Above all, you should be able to be your authentic self around this person. You should not feel like you need to hide anything from them, and if you are actually authentic, you will not be able to hide anything once trust is instilled. You should want to be completely open and honest with them, as this is the basis of a solid and genuine relationship between two people.

With that said, you should not want to change your partner in any way. If they are able to be their authentic self with you, you should not want to alter anything about them. When you come together in a relationship, part of the beauty is learning and experiencing new and exciting things. If there is anything that stands in the way of your values, then this relationship may ultimately not work in the long-term.

If there are any problems or arguments which may come to pass, maintain respect for each other by not talking over each other or dismissing each other's ideas. Remember that you are a team who should be able to work through any difficulties together. Of course, not everything is going to be right and perfect in any relationship. There will still be disagreements and problems. However, when you and your partner are able to work together to come up with mutually-beneficial solutions consistently, then you will certainly know that you are meant to be together.

When you are sure of yourself and can be yourself, your partner will appreciate you for being real, honest, and open with them. It will create a bond that will last a long time. Of course, all relationships need continuous work. Nothing is ever a "done deal," and you should want to continue to grow and share with them to continue to deepen your relationship over time.

CHAPTER 10

Relax, Stop Worrying Too Much and Appreciate What You Have

Worrying And Overthinking

Have you heard the song "High as Fuck" by Jon Lajoie? If you haven't, then go ahead and look it up. You're welcome. Anyways, there's a line in there that says, "You need snacks so you walk to the corner store/ But you're scared that they would know you're high/ So you walk around the block to buy some time."

It's so funny because it's so accurate. As a young person, I was high many times, and that's exactly what happened to me most of the time.

I remember cruising around town with my friend Ron. We were high and just driving around the lettuce fields of Salinas, California, venting stress, and talking about random stuff when suddenly, I felt like having a burger.

So, Ron drove to a Carl's Jr. which was the closest fast-food chain to where we were. Then, as soon as we got there, I told him to go to In-N-Out instead, which got him a little upset, but he drove us there anyway.

When we got there, he parked out front and told me to go ahead and order while he waited in the car. I was scared to get out of the car. I was scared that the people inside would know that I was high. So I asked Ron to go through the drive-thru instead, telling him about what I was worried about.

This was when he snapped.

"Dude, you know what? Do you think people in there check out everyone who walks in to see if they're high?"

To which I replied, "Dude, my eyes are red, and we don't have eye drops."

"Fuck eyedrops! Nobody in there is spending their time checking out everyone's eyes! You know what? I think half the people in there right now are high! Just fucking go! Nobody gives a shit if you're high or not. Just go in there and order your damn burger!"

What, did you think that people hang out at inn' out and make a hobby out of spotting who's high and who's not? Nobody has time for that!

Believe me; this was just a small part of it. He must have spent half an hour yelling at me inside the car. If I wasn't stoned, I'm sure I would have had a panic attack or something just from seeing how angry he was. As it was, I just let him let it out. Then, when I finally decided to get out, he told me that we would just go to the drive-thru anyway.

Ron is a really good friend of mine, and he's a great guy, but he does have anger issues. But anger issues aside, he was right. Nobody cared if I was high. I could have just walked in there and got my burger and saved myself from a half-hour-long tirade.

I'm sure that you don't have to be high to worry about things that don't matter. When I was still on the dating scene, I would always worry too much about every single detail, making things more complicated than it should have been. I tried to analyze every gesture and word that my dates expressed in real-time to try to see how interested they were in me or to try to come up with a plan, also in real-time, on how to move and respond to make them like me more.

Of course, doing it like that, trying to calculate everything, ends up making it feel forced and awkward and usually doesn't result in a second date.

There's nothing wrong with trying to analyze and plan things, but sometimes, things are a lot less complicated than you think.

When you find yourself overanalyzing things and driving yourself crazy thinking about every possibility including everything that could go wrong, or every solution to every possible problem, maybe it's time to stop for a moment and take a deep breath. Actually, that helps a lot. Try counting your breaths. It should help you re-focus your thoughts.

You probably want everything to be perfect. It's okay to want things to be perfect. Who doesn't want things to go exactly the way they want them to? But the thing is, you can't keep wasting time and energy on trying to make everything perfect.

Feeling worried about something is natural, and I believe that it's part of our defense mechanism. We worry because we are smart enough to anticipate potential threats. A healthy amount of worrying is good as it lets us prepare.

Worrying becomes a problem when we let our worries become irrational and debilitating. It becomes a problem when you spend a great deal of time worrying and overthinking that you fail to act and miss out on real opportunities.

Are you familiar with the law of diminishing returns? It says that there is a point at which the level of profits or benefits gained is less than the amount of money or energy invested. In simple terms, this means that there's only so much you can do that's worth your time and energy. After a certain point, all the extra effort you put into worrying and trying to fix every single issue becomes a waste of time.

Learn To Appreciate What You Have

Have you ever ruined things for yourself because you were overthinking or became an idiot, acting based on the wrong assumptions?- I certainly have, and it royally sucked once I realized how wrong I was.

Back in high school, I used to have this thing where I looked at the phone directory and would dial numbers that were within easy traveling distance. If the person who answered was someone who sounded like a young lady, I would try to get a conversation going. Basically, I was cold-calling for female phone pals. If you're a millennial, you probably won't get the concept because this was before cellphones became a common thing for everyone to have. Eventually, after talking to them for a while, we agree to meet at a certain place and time and wear specific colors of clothes so we can approach each other and formally meet. I don't know what it's called in the US, but in the Philippines, we called it an "eyeball."

If things went well during the meeting, you could decide to take the relationship further, or if it didn't go well or if you weren't each other's types, then you part ways and usually stop talking.

I've been on the receiving end of someone not showing up to an eyeball, just sitting there by myself for an hour without ever meeting the person. I've also been guilty of not showing up to meet the girl when I see them first and determine that they're not my type.

Sometimes, the girls I've been talking to wouldn't agree to an eyeball, but they would give me the number of one of their friends and introduce me on the phone. That was how I met this girl I'll call Jasmine. She was introduced to me by one of my phone pals and screwing things up with her will always be the biggest regrets of my life.

Jasmine had a cute voice, and she was very nice. Best of all, she was down to talk on the phone for hours almost every day. We had so much fun talking that our thing lasted for years, from mid-high school to early college. We talked about a lot of things, including personal stuff and became really close.

The funny thing is, we never really thought of ever meeting until about a couple of years if I'm not mistaken.

Honestly, I stopped caring about how she looked. After years of talking, she had become one of my best friends, even when I haven't met her in person. Finally, when we decided to meet, I was pleasantly surprised because she was really beautiful, but by then, I already had a girlfriend, and she'd become a really good friend that I didn't even consider asking out because I was afraid of ruining our friendship.

We later ended up attending the same school in college, but we were in different classes with entirely different schedules, so we rarely met in school.

Eventually, I became single again and a little while after that, I decided to ask her out, and she quickly agreed to go out with me. Going out with her was so much fun. By this time we already knew a lot about each other, so things went really smoothly, and it was almost a sure thing that should have lasted for years and maybe would have ended up with a wedding and cute kids.

Unfortunately, that's not what happened, and it was all because I was an idiot. We were supposed to go out on a date one afternoon after classes. I waited for her to finish then got her from class and were on the way out of campus when suddenly, this friend of hers comes and asks for her help in riding the bus home.

This friend of hers was a rich girl who never took public transportation even once in her life, and that afternoon her driver had some kind of issue, and nobody was available to pick her up on short notice. Jasmine, being the kind person that she was, asked me to cancel the date and helped her friend.

My mistake? First, I was an idiot for not thinking of going with them. Instead, I got upset and let them go without much of a reaction.

Second, I was an arrogant fool. Remember the time when I thought I was cool? It was around that time, and Jasmine was one of the only real friends I had. But, because I wanted to act cool, I stopped talking to her and I quit dating her because I wanted to project that I could have any woman I wanted and that when she decided to pick helping her friend over going out on a date with me, she missed out on having her chance with me.

I was a stupid, arrogant, dumb, piece-of-shit idiot. I spent a lot of nights after that in heavy drinking because I really wanted Jasmine, but I wanted to keep my "image," which I didn't realize back then was really nothing. Remember, I thought I was cool. I was worried about people thinking that I was letting a girl disrespect me. She was one of the very few people who knew the real me, and I threw it all away of worrying about my stupid reputation, which I was also too stupid to realize didn't really exist. Nobody respected me. Nobody thought I was awesome - except Jasmine, who had been my friend and stuck with me for years. If I was supposed to worry about something, I should have worried about her and her friend going home.

One night, about a couple of months later, I got drunk and decided to call her. By then, I could sense the disappointment in her tone, and even then, she listened to me blame her for picking her friend of a date with me. After I was done talking, she calmly told me, "You're really not as cool and attractive as you think you are. You wasted everything. Don't talk to me again."

That was the end. It was beautiful, and it could have been something that could have lasted a very long time, but I ruined it all for nothing. If only I appreciated having her instead of worrying more about how other people would think of me.

I was selfish and expected too much from myself and other people. I tried to control everything, and I ended up losing more than I have ever won.

That's usually what happens if you spend all your time worrying about every little thing and focusing on the things that you're missing instead of appreciating the things that you already have.

If you're reading this book right now, then it means that you're already doing better than about half the world's population. Why? Because you have enough money to buy a book off an internet store and have own a device that let you access the internet and place that order.

Many people in the world still don't own a computer, a tablet, or a smartphone. Some places don't even have internet access.

I know you probably have problems and I'm not saying that they don't matter. All I'm saying is that there are things that you take for granted that to other people could mean the world so you should appreciate the things you have and just relax a little.

CHAPTER 11

Continuously Improve Yourself
and Become the Best Person
You Can Be

I f you paid attention to my stories, you'd see how far I've come since being that kid who got free snacks in order to have friends.

Now, I'm a writer publishing books for others to read, and I'm sharing my story to the world, hoping that other people can benefit from my experiences and the lessons I have learned.

Also, I'm an entrepreneur who has had my hand on different businesses and has failed a lot more times than I ever succeeded, but I know I'll get there if I just keep pushing.

At the time of writing this book, I'm also taking a few courses on how to launch a successful Youtube channel, and also in my queue of courses is how to Podcast. I guess I still got that little kid inside me who wants people to pay attention to him and love him, only this time I'm attempting on doing it on a much larger scale. I want to be a household brand, and I want to reach and help more people with my stories.

The point I'm trying to make here is that we humans have a lot of potential. We have the ability to learn and adapt. We can become almost anything if we put our mind to it.

Whatever your dreams are of becoming, you're free, and you have the potential to reach that goal if you are willing to put in the work and time required to get there.

There is no limit to improving yourself. You can always look for new things to learn and more ways to apply the knowledge that you already possess in order to improve yourself.

Just because you learned to love yourself just the way you are doesn't mean that you can slack off and stay exactly where you are. It's a big world out there, and there's a lot of things you can explore and do to make your life more fun and meaningful.

The Secret To Happiness

If you're reading this book, chances are, you want certain things to happen in your life like make new friends or be in a relationship with someone who loves and appreciates you. So what happens once you have all that? Do you just stop?

Based on my own observations, being truly happy in life isn't simply about reaching a single goal, but it's in the continuous cycle of finding new goals, working toward those goals, and finally reaching them. Then, it's on to the next set of goals.

That's why, for example, a lot of people buy the latest phone model this year, only to replace them next year when the next latest model comes out.

If you're one of those people who will keep using the same phone for years as long as it's still working then good for you, but have you ever noticed that there are things that you used to be really happy and excited about that you now take for granted?

I'm not saying that you can't be contented with what you are and with what you have. The feeling of contentment is something I also understand like how I'm contented with my one daughter, and it doesn't matter to me whether I have another child in the future or not. I'm happy with my relationship with my only daughter. But the thing is that she will keep growing up and eventually she will have a family of her own and I won't get to take care of her anymore. I'll also grow old one day, and I may no longer spend time with her as much as I want.

One way or another, our relationship will change whether I like it or not. I can't stop her from growing up, and I can't keep her with me forever because she's her own person and her happiness isn't always going to be something that I alone can provide.

So, the best thing I can do for myself is to adapt and learn. As my daughter grows up and beings to have a life of her own, I too have to find a new approach to keep our relationship healthy. One day she'll no longer have the time to visit me as often as I would like so I would either have to be the one to visit her when she is off work or when she's not available, I have to find other things for me to do to have fun and keep myself from missing her.

It's kind of sad now that I think about it, but it's just the way it's going to go. It's also true not only with my relationship with my daughter but also with all my other relationships, including the one I have with myself. That's because the world is dynamic, things are constantly changing, and we are all steadily evolving. The world doesn't stop just because you've reached your goals or finally got what you've always wanted.

Setting Goals

If you want to keep feeling happy then you have to keep finding things for you to improve and you have to find yourself new goals and milestones to work towards and that's why this chapter is all about continuously improving yourself and being the best person you can be.

The first step then is identifying the things about yourself that need improvement, as well as figuring out what direction you want to take with your life.

Once you find the areas which you need to improve, the next step is to set goals towards achieving those areas of improvement that you have identified.

The next thing you have to do then is to come up with a plan of action. If the idea of making plans feels overwhelming, don't worry, most people do not know how to go about making plans. Just keep it simple in the meantime like right now, your plan is to reach your goals. You can always build on your plan as you learn more and receive new information. When you have a plan in place, it is much easier to be motivated towards accomplishing your goals.

New to Goal Setting? Try S.M.A.R.T.!

When you are first starting out in goal setting, it is best to start with small and attainable goals. You will still want to set personal goals for yourself to continue to push yourself to your limits. Think outside of the box and expand your personal talents such as learning a foreign language, taking up a new hobby, or even learning how to play a musical instrument.

Consider making goals where you can learn more about yourself and how you interact with the world around you and challenge yourself to reach those goals. Working towards reaching those goals could let you grow in ways that you would not have thought possible without them in place.

It should help continue to broaden your horizons, helping you come in contact with different types of people and strengthening your body and mind. This, in turn, will help you bring out your hidden talents as you will be utilizing them to learn new things.

A proven method known as the S.M.A.R.T. goal process is an excellent way to start goal planning. The acronym stands for Specific, Measurable, Actionable, Reasonable, and Time-bound. It was the idea behind the paper written by George T. Doran by the name of There's a S.M.A.R.T. Way to Write Management's Goals and Objectives. Even though this was written nearly four decades ago, it still is a proven way to create a solid plan that you will follow through.

The following are the sections of the goal process, which you will focus on to reach your personal goals.

Specific – This is the part of the plan which is designed to be unambiguous, clear, and well-defined. When you are able to create a plan which follows these guidelines, you will have a much greater chance of accomplishing your goal. When you start to construct a solid goal, you will want to think about the following questions:

Who is going to be involved in this goal?

What exactly do I want to achieve?

Where is this goal going to be accomplished?

When would I want to attain this goal?

Why do I want to accomplish this goal?

Now, as an example, let's say that you want to lose weight and you set that as your goal.

Using the example that you would like to lose weight, you will need to make this goal more developed and focused. An example of this would be that you would want to lose 10lbs. Also, you will add something like in order to achieve it; you'll exercise daily at the local gym while starting to eat healthier foods. When you create a more focused idea behind your goal, you will have a better direction on how to achieve your personal goal, and you will be more likely to get the end result you desire.

Measurable – This is the section in which you are going to be able to measure your progress as you work towards your ultimate goal. If you do not have this in place, you are not going to know if you are on track with realizing your goal. Let us measure the goals with losing weight while asking the following questions:

How much weight do I need to lose to feel happier and be healthier?

How will I know when I have reached my final goal?

What indicators am I going to use to see if I am progressing with my goal of losing 10lbs?

You will want to put a reasonable measurement on success. Try your best to not have a very high expectation for results, at least at the beginning because you might end up setting yourself up for failure. For example, you can set your weekly goal to be one or two pounds lost per week. This leads into the next section of the goal.

Achievable – Your personal goal must be realistic so that you will be able to attain the final result you want. This is a part of the plan that is flexible so that you can push yourself to the limit when necessary or adjust it at a comfortable level for you. The questions you will ask yourself during this phase are:

Do I possess the capability and resources to accomplish my goal? If I do not, what exactly do I need to achieve my goal?

Have other people accomplished the same goal of weight loss?

Of course, other people have been successful in weight loss, and it may take a little creativity to lose weight if you do not have the means to spend money on expensive equipment or a gym membership. This is a point where you need to be honest with yourself without destroying your opportunity to lose weight successfully.

Realistic – Some people put unrealistic expectations on themselves. Just because someone else may have lost 20 pounds in two months does not mean this is going to work for you. You need to be honest with yourself so that you do not set yourself up for failure. To make sure you are on the right track, ask yourself these questions:

Is my goal of weight loss within my reach and realistic?

Can I reach this goal given the resources and time that I have allotted?

Am I able to commit to what it takes to lose weight in the time I have set?

It is okay if you went past your comfort zone early on by setting an unrealistic goal. This is your chance to tweak the plan so that you are not going to get frustrated along your journey to lose the weight you wish. Remember not to be too hard on yourself and just keep moving forward.

Time-bound – This last section of the goal is going to make sure that you are accountable. You are going to need to set a date by which you are going to start working towards your goal and when you are supposed to finish. If you do not create a specific time-frame to work on your goal, it will simply be put off until you feel it is convenient. The questions you will need to ask yourself to ensure you have set a good schedule are:

Does my goal of weight loss have a specific deadline?

What are my milestones or how much should I have lost by each of them?

You will also want to incorporate how much time you want to spend days on exercising and losing weight. This will keep you accountable each day as you are working towards the end date of your goal. This step will finalize your overall goal with all the details.

To make yourself more successful at the plan you choose, you need to focus on the why and how of your goal. When you have your answers to these questions, along with the instructions of the S.M.A.R.T. goal plan, you will have an ample amount of the competency, confidence, and motivation required to succeed at your new personal goal.

Your "Why"

When you set a goal, you need to have a firm reason for why you want to accomplish this goal. The reason behind your "why" should be a personal one. The more personal the "why," the more successful you will be. You also want to be as detailed as possible.

As an example, your "why" for losing weight can be "I want to look and feel great when I go on my dream vacation this summer" as this is a reason personal to you. On the contrary, "my doctor said that I should lose weight for health reasons" is the "why" of your physician not you. As long as your "why" is of a personal nature, you will find that you will be more determined to reach your goal.

Your "How"

The "how" of your goal is the different methods and tactics you'll be using to ensure your goal is achieved. You will want to take your overall goal and split it up into smaller steps to work on your goal in bite-sized pieces. This will keep you more focused and help you avoid frustration and getting overwhelmed. It will also help you allocate the different steps on a daily or weekly basis to give yourself a straight path to walk towards realizing your goal.

In addition to these steps, you can make it even more concrete by writing a mission statement. This will help you to visualize, on paper, your entire S.M.A.R.T. goal. You should write a statement like the following:

I will (write your clear goal fully) by (the date by which you want to achieve your goal) because (your "why").

State your intention clearly so that you never lose sight of why you created your goal in the first place.

Remember to not go over the top with your goal setting when you are just starting. You will want to build confidence in your abilities first before you start to go after something major.

Try BHAG for Life-Changing Goals

Many famous people and companies incorporate the idea of BHAG goals, which stands for Big Hairy Audacious Goal. This acronym was coined by James Collins and Jerry Porras in their book called "Built to Last: Successful Habits of Visionary Companies." The idea behind this type of long-term goal is to create a result that drastically changes where you are today.

Even though it started out as a business idea, individuals such as Arnold Schwarzenegger incorporated it saying that he wanted to become a big movie star after his career in bodybuilding came to an end. There is no reason why you shouldn't be able to take the same approach with your life if you are looking for a grand change.

When you are creating a BHAG, you need to envision a goal which is compelling, clear, and will create a tremendous amount of inspiration. You are going to aspire to be your ideal self. It is going to be focused, but it will consist of several smaller steps to achieve the larger goal. Your BHAG should be able to excite you to be more creative as well as push you to achieve more success in your life.

Creating a strategy in achieving your BHAG is the way to successfully reaching it. Your strategy would be your overall plan. You will be motivated to move forward as your strategy guides you in a direct path to realizing your goal. Let us use the example of a BGAG being Complete Financial Freedom. Your strategy should be something like "make an X amount of money per month" to ensure you do not need to worry about finances. To know what this number should be, you will need to set up a monthly budget to list your expenses as well as extras that may come up unexpectedly.

Next, the next step would be to identify or develop your tactics. Tactics are different from strategies in the sense that the strategies are of a larger, more general scope, whereas your tactics are the actual specific moves that you will be taking. There are many tactics that are required for one BHAG, and this is the part of the process where you can instill your creativity. The possibilities are endless, and it is up to you to think outside of the box and to be open to any and all ideas.

Picking up from the strategy of making an X amount of money per month, you will need to come up with a plan to bring in those extra funds. Your tactics can be "saving X amount of money every day" or "not using your credit card. "Do you have the time to take on an extra job, a side project, or put in extra hours at work? Perhaps there are things around your home that you do not use or need any longer that you can sell to help buffer your initial income. Maybe you are not getting the money that you are worth at your current job. It may be worth looking at other opportunities where you can make more money for the same amount of time that you are working now.

When you employ any of these tactics to support your goal, they will, in turn, push you towards your final goal. The tactics can also be broken down further by creating daily actions which can result in habits. Let's say you want to make another $1000 per month. You would simply divide that number by the number of days in the month to know how much more money you need to make on a daily basis to reach your goal. It will then become a natural habit to work towards.

Once you have your tactics and daily habits planned out, the next step with your BHAG is to set a milestone, which is either set by a specific amount of time or a certain interval, such as $250 or $500 more a month earned in regards to the example. Whatever your goal is, it needs to be broken down into smaller and attainable goals which you can reward yourself for.

If you set a milestone, and you are not doing as well as you had hoped, do not lose hope. This gives you the opportunity to evaluate the ways that your plan is and is not working. From here, you should be able to improve the tactics within the plan. Depending on how far off you were from your mark, you will either need to make small tweaks or significant adjustments. If you are determined enough to reach your goal, it is worth a little trial and error to get there. Use the flexibility of the plan set to your advantage in this case.

It can also help to get at least one other person to have as an accountability partner. This person should be someone who will be able to push you and give you feedback to further improve your tactics and plans. They may be able to give you a different perspective and give you further ideas on how to push forward towards your goal.

Of course, this accountability partner should also have your best interests at heart and even better if they have a personal interest in you achieving your goal. This person or people that you choose should not have any hesitation to speak up in case they see a fault in your tactics, and they should be available on a regular basis to check in with the progress of your BHAG.

As with any long-term goal, you are not necessarily going to see results quickly. You must trust the process and continue to hold on to the determination you have to reach the end of your goal plan. When you are focused on the overall journey of your BHAG, it will become an integral part of your life for the time being, which is the point. You are always continuing towards the change, which the goal is expected to bring to your life.

Yes, your BHAG is going to take an immense amount of work. You can compare it to raising a child because of the necessary attention and energy that it requires to come to the end result. However, continue to work the system you have put into place, and you will see that the payoffs are worth the amount of effort you put in.

P.A.C.T. Will Keep You On Track

Another way to ensure you stay on track towards your goal is to follow the P.A.C.T., which is a promise to yourself. The acronym stands for Patience, Action, Consistency, and Time. This can be used in conjunction with either S.M.A.R.T. or B.H.A.G. to keep you focused.

Patience – As with all things worth having, you will need to be patient with yourself while realizing your goals. If you do not possess patience, you will simply give up when things get hard. You will gradually start to build up your confidence as you start to see your tactics showing results. You should then start to trust your system and allow the time it requires to come to completion.

Action – Of course, this step is needed for anything you try to achieve in your life. If you do not take action, nothing will happen. Continue to have a daily task to perform so that you are always in a forward motion towards your goal. Make these actions direct and specific, such as "run for three miles," and put them on a calendar. Remember to keep true to your steps and make these daily tasks non-negotiable.

Consistency – This step goes hand in hand with Action because the tactics need to be consistent. You cannot take a break when you are working on a goal. You need to be relentless and determined to reach your goal, no matter what. Consistency helps you to continue to be true to yourself while you are working towards your goal.

Time – This is already an aspect which is included in both goal plans mentioned earlier. It cannot be stressed enough how important timing is for accomplishing your goals. It is this aspect which drives the whole process. If you do not respect your start date, milestones or end date, you will not be able to achieve your goal in the time you have set.

When you use all of these tools to your advantage to create a solid goal plan, you should be able to accomplish your personal goal with great success. With a detailed road map in your hands, there is no excuse to not stay on the path straight to realizing your goal.

Striving to be the very best person that you can possibly be is the best gift that you can give yourself once you've learned to appreciate and love yourself. It is also a part of self-love because you push yourself to become a better version of yourself. When you decide to work towards being your best self, your life will be enriched in ways that you could not imagine. You might also discover that you are capable of great things that you never even expected of yourself.

Final Words

In all situations where you are working on improving yourself, never accept failure as an option. With this mindset, you will be able to accomplish anything that you set out to complete. Understand that there is always a solution to any problem, obstacle, or challenge that comes along your path, so there is no reason to ever give up.

There is a reason that you got this book. Maybe it was curiosity or seeing how someone else was able to finally learn from different life experiences persuaded you to do the same. Maybe it was already your goal to make an improvement in your life. Or perhaps you just realized that nothing was working out for you in the way that you had hoped.

Whatever the case may be, you have the power of knowledge in your hands to be able to make tangible and real changes within yourself and your life. There is no going back to the way that you lived your life before with what you have read in my book.

If you bring the determination and drive that you need to succeed to the table, there is nothing other than yourself that can stand in your way. With all the different methods, directions, and advice that is loaded in this book, you can set yourself on the right path. There is always a way, and there is always hope.

It is your choice each day when you wake up to make it a better day than it was yesterday. There is always room for improvement. With this mindset, you will accomplish everything you set out to achieve, and you will see massive changes in your life.

I hope you now understand that there are awesome rewards that lie in store for you when you start to give the real you a chance to shine and be seen and appreciated. When you live your own life on your own terms, you get to write the script. You are the one in control.

If you still feel like you do not know where to start, look in the mirror and tell yourself one good quality, strength, or accomplishment that you have achieved thus far. Let this be your mantra until you are able to add more to the list. Start making small positive changes like eating better or going after your dream job or smoking a little less each day.

Any effort that you put into improving yourself and becoming more real is a step in the right direction. If you need a support system, find a buddy who can help support you mentally through some of the harder tasks. Let them be your cheerleader as you continue to strive to be the best that you can possibly be.

Once you get your footing, start practicing the methods in this book as soon as possible. Why wait? There are only good things to come when you are able to be more confident within yourself and stop putting all your effort into this fake persona that you have hidden yourself behind. Let yourself shine with all your unique qualities. Why would you want to hide your awesomeness from the world?

Practice your communication skills every chance you get. This will not only strengthen them, but you will also create lasting and memorable bonds with those that you meet and work with. Be honest at all times, as well as kind. You will go far with this type of mindset. Also, let me remind you about that quick guide I mentioned earlier to help you make a great first impression and start meaningful conversations. You can get from my website at https://johnfernando.com.

And speaking of your mind, be sure to keep a handle on your thoughts throughout this entire process. It can be difficult at times if you have self-esteem issues or a negative dialogue constantly spinning around in your head. But keep this in mind - nothing is permanent.

Change always occurs, and there will be an end, especially when your mind is bent on it.

Do not be so hard on yourself through this process. Many of these aspects I have written about have been learned over decades of time. There is no magic pill that you can take or quick fix method that will turn your life around in one fell swoop.

There is always something to inspire you. Whatever or whoever that person is, let them know that they mean that much to you. Not only will they be flattered, but they will also likely become another cheerleader for you while you are on your personal authenticity journey. You can never have enough people rooting for you on your side, believe me.

But even if you do not have the "rah rahs" coming from the stands, muster up the courage and strength within yourself to know that you are able to make a difference in your life today, even in the slightest bit. Every day, keep building upon what you worked on the day before. You will start to notice all of the small changes adding up to where they are becoming habits without you realizing it. It really does not take a lot to start, but you'll need a plan to keep going and stay on track.

If I was able to be happy with myself and make real friends who don't need me to pretend to be someone else, you could do it too. Just set a daily goal, stick to it, and keep it up. It is that simple. Do not ever let yourself take a day off from being yourself and from working on consistently improving yourself. Again, no one is perfect, and there may be things about you that you're not proud of, but don't let those things stop you from bringing out the great things inside you. You are unique, and you are awesome, never stop believing in yourself.

Good luck! And know that I will be on the sidelines, rooting for you.